The American Idiom

William Carlos Williams
Harold Norse

The American Idiom

A Correspondence

Edited by John J. Wilson

Bright Tyger Press

Cover Photograph of William Carlos Williams
©1990 by John D. Schiff

Cover Photograph of Harold Norse in 1958
©1990 by Harold Norse

The correspondence of William Carlos Williams is published by arrangement
with New Directions Publishing Corp., New York, agents for
William Eric Williams, and Paul H. Williams.

The original letters of William Carlos Williams and Florence Williams to Harold Norse
are in the Harold Norse Collection, Lilly Library, Indiana University, Bloomington IN.
Photo images used by permission.

The original letters of Harold Norse to William Carlos Williams are in the Collection of
American Literature, Beinecke Rare Book and Manuscript Library, Yale University.
Photo images used by permission.

The correspondence in this book previously appeared in *Helix*.

LIBRARY OF CONGRESS CATALOGING-IN-PUBLICATION DATA

William Carlos Williams & Harold Norse
The American Idiom

1. Williams, William Carlos and Norse, Harold—Correspondence.
2. Authors, American—20th Century—Correspondence. I. Title.
Printed in the United States of America

First Edition 1990
ISBN: 0-944378-79-X
HARDCOVER ISBN: 0-944378-80-3

Cover Design and Layout by Earl Flewellen

Bright Tyger Press, 537 Jones Street, Suite 263, San Francisco, CA 91402.

PREFACE

I remember attending a talk by Allen Tate in 1956 at the American Library in Florence. He compared the two contending "baseball teams" of American writing to the "palefaces" and "redskins" (coined by Philip Rahv), the former on the Henry James model, the latter of the Walt Whitman "barbaric yawp" type. "Our team has won," he purred with smug satisfaction. "We palefaces have kept the trophy for two decades." Ironically, at that very moment Allen Ginsberg's *Howl* was creating an international sensation; despite establishment attacks on the new Beat writers, the redskins had won the pennant.

The only other remark I recall, in an otherwise forgettable speech, were words to this effect: "Two geniuses, Ezra Pound and T. S. Eliot, created the new writing which led to the New Criticism, *our* school." He completely ignored the third genius, William Carlos Williams, who had been creating the most important change—away *from* pedantic intellectualism. The three geniuses of my generation who were making the next major (postmodern) change, begun by William Carlos Williams, were Allen Ginsberg, Jack Kerouac, and William S. Burroughs.

At the time only formalist poetry was taken seriously. Most of it was technique without passion, cold, bloodless, neoclassical. Poets wrote to the metronome in iambics, with inert forms and literary diction; irony replaced feeling. Now many poets who teach use the best elements of dissimilar ways of writing, but in the forties and fifties mentioning Walt Whitman was heresy, Gertrude Stein was regarded as a joke, and academic critics were the sole arbiters of taste. Ezra Pound, for all his detestable political views, was one of the few rebellious voices they admired. But his old friend, William Carlos Williams, despite major awards and honors, remained an outsider.

When I began my career in the forties, the academic school of white, male, elitist, middle-class professor-poets held sway: Allen Tate, John Crowe Ransom and Robert Penn Warren (all Southern gentlemen) led the New Critics and taught in the universities. Passion and personality were outlawed, resulting for the most part in constipated expression. There were no prominent Black, Asian, Hispanic or Native American names and few Jews, notably Laura Riding, who had influenced them *and* the young Auden, and then became the mentor of Robert Graves. In my letter of 8 September 1960 to Williams I said, "I was a...victim of...the timid, fearful milieu of that time when poets agreed with Auden that 'poetry makes nothing happen.'" Ultimately, Robert Lowell, John Berryman and Sylvia Plath, trained by the New Critics, broke from the mold in their later work—Lowell attributed his *Life Studies* to the influence of William Carlos Williams and Sylvia Plath attributed her breakthrough in *Ariel* to *Life Studies*. Thus Williams, whose influence on Allen Ginsberg led to *Howl* (for which he wrote the preface) turned the tide of American poetry by opening the door for both the new Beat Generation and the established academic poets.

This, of course, was not recognized for years. When he wasn't being ignored Williams was harshly censured as a wild man, about both of which he never ceased to complain. While the academics modeled writing on the past, the English tradition, he stressed the present with its immediacy, cacophany, ugliness and disorder; he detested rhyme, meters, fixed forms, and baroque high style, insisting on colloquial American speech, associational and collage techniques. He restructured the line in what he called "broken style," or "loose verses," and shifted the emphasis from formalist to experimental, expanding the horizons of poetry, which Pound in his snobbish, bookish way had begun. Even his subject matter, in prose and verse, opened out to poor, working class immigrants whom, as a pediatrician, he treated—Polish, Swedish, Irish, German, Jewish, Italian, Black women. Their illiterate broken English comprised one aspect of his revolution in the sound of poetry.

In the forties, like Ginsberg, whom I had met in 1944 when he was an 18-year-old freshman at Columbia University, I was struggling against the prevailing current. Role models were few. I worked on accentual measures and read some of Williams' poetry, but wasn't overwhelmed until, in 1951, in an enthusiastic letter, Williams singled out a poem of mine and encouraged me to go all the way into the *terra incognita* of the new. I was teaching college and working for my master's degree at New York University when our correspondence began. My first response to his letter was written five years before Ginsberg wrote *Howl;* my last letters, from 1959 to 1963 (some are missing after 1961), issued from the Beat Hotel in Paris, where, with William Burroughs and Gregory Corso, I experimented with cut-up language and techniques that Williams, had he lived, would have applauded. In 1956 he wrote the preface for my Belli translations and in 1959 acknowledged my breakthrough in poetry. Unarguably, he had opened my eyes.

When I received his first letter out of the blue, it was a heady, exhilarating experience and just what I needed, for I was groping in the dark alone, unaided. This is what the correspondence is about—a master-disciple relationship in unexplored territory. We argued, quarreled, disagreed, and at times contradicted ourselves. We veered from enthusiasm to sour grapes about other poets and writers, and even about each other, and then reversed our positions. It may not seem so remarkable now, but at the time Williams' singleminded pursuit of American speech and rhythms true to the flow of thought, as suggested by Whitman, was revolutionary. He shifted the balance of power from elitism to populism, enabling poetry to be practiced, read and performed widely for large audiences. The base was further broadened by the enormous impact of Ginsberg and the Beats, who influenced rock and folk singers. Considering the ramifications, Williams is probably the best thing since Whitman that ever happened to American poetry—and, certainly, to me.

Williams died before the full consequences of his work were appreciated. He changed not only poetry but American cultural history in the second half of the 20th Century. The letters reveal the unflagging devotion and uncompromising dedication of an aging, ailing major poet to an idea that he would fight for to the last breath, and also his keen desire to bring out the potential of a young aspiring poet in whom he believed. Equally important, the letters also reveal the battleground between the two forces in U.S. poetry that, as valid traditions in their own right, contend within the work of one young poet torn between them while attempting, in his own life-work, to reconcile them.

*   *   *

I have resisted the temptation to delete words and expressions that I would no longer use, such as "girl" for woman, for example, and have deleted only two lines that might offend living persons of both genders. Not only Feminist women's writing but, also growing out of social change that began with writers and artists in the fifties and sixties, powerful Black, Asian, Hispanic, Native American and Jewish writers have influenced me since then, and continue to do so. And for the first time since classical Greece and Rome, Gay and Lesbian poetry has emerged openly, with a bold, new awareness and pioneering spirit.

It was the crucial correspondence in my life—like being trained by a Zen master who bypassed the domination of the intellect and got to the now-experience, beginning a new line of succession. Without Williams we probably wouldn't have had *Howl, Life Studies, Ariel* and *The Dream Poems*.Nor would we have had this rough-and-tumble exchange of letters, with its passionate outbursts of feeling, its unguarded spontaneity, its swift illuminations. It was new ground and we wrote straight from the heart, the head and various unmentionable parts of the body.

I would like to remind the reader that these letters were not intended for publication and that many opinions I held then I no longer hold. Since repatriation to the United States in 1968 I have found the work of Olson, Creeley, Bukowski, Levertov, Ignatow and, above all, Ginsberg, to be of major significance in the creation of a new prosody, thanks to Williams' ground-breaking work for the American idiom. As an expatriate I could not unreservedly appreciate their achievement, feeling estranged, at the time, from the American scene, and mostly unfamiliar with their work. Despite some ill-tempered thrusts in 1958 at Ginsberg and Kerouac, by 1959 (see my letter of 1 June 1960) I fully appreciated the enormous innovative changes they brought about, and defended them against Williams himself (who was probably galled, as I was, by the vast media attention they were receiving), and I haven't wavered from that opinion in thirty years.

I was tempted to rewrite phrases and sentences, change a word here and there, but for the most part refrained, leaving awkward structure, sloppy sentences, weird grammar. Williams was "anti-poetic" and I was learning to be. If some of it sounds banal and crude, so be it. We valued impromptu expression and eschewed literary posturing. A revolution in style was in the making, and Williams was its mentor. Successful beyond belief, it has proven its vitality by its power to endure, especially because of Ginsberg, Kerouac, and Burroughs.

Finally, I hope these straightforward, candid letters will have for contemporary readers the interest that, in a more personal way, they have for me. Surely, they will take their place as the last, but not least, of the historic correspondences between Williams and younger poets of the fifties whose work he espoused before critics came around to it.

—Harold Norse
May 1990, San Francisco

INTRODUCTION

At least since the writing of *Paterson 4* (1949-51), wherein the young Allen Ginsberg becomes the literary son to Dr. Paterson, William Carlos Williams had been on the lookout for young poets to carry on with the work that he felt had only begun. Charles Olson, Robert Creeley, Cid Corman, Denise Levertov, David Ignatow, in fact a burgeoning entourage, sought out Williams' advice and support in the fifties and carried on a correspondence with him through the decade, and Williams gladly accommodated them.

Harold Norse, like all these poets, was not then well known, but at times Williams placed in him his highest hopes. "You're the best young poet of your generation," Norse remembers Williams writing in the letter (now lost) which came to Norse "out of the blue." In a letter to me, Norse described how he came to know Williams when "a group of young poets [including Paul Blackburn, Louis Dudek, Raymond Souster, John Kasper, and, Norse thinks, James Merrill] asked me to join a round robin, each submitting two or three poems and criticizing each other's work. The whole batch was to end with Pound at St. Eliz. & Williams in Rutherford. Williams chose 'The Railroad Yard' [published under the title 'Warnings & Promises' in *The Undersea Mountain*], wrote me out of the blue from the hospital (first stroke) singling me out... The friendship began through this. I had never spoken to him or written to him before. He recommended the poem to Laughlin for ND and L. published it. Pound ignored the entire bunch."

Years later, when trying to explain his disappointment in

the metrical, rhyming poems that Norse had sent to him over the past two years, Williams said, "I don't mind telling you I was beginning to think you were lost to me forever. It broke my heart because I counted on you as being the one guy who would carry the battle without flagging deep into the enemy territory [more or less, traditional English metric]" (see letter of 13 June 1960). Williams' pugnacity toward the English tradition, especially as it was embraced by T. S. Eliot and those poets who followed him, is now common knowledge. But still too often Williams is viewed as a father figure adopted by the "new American poets" of the fifties, when *he* was trying to rally young allies who would "fight," or go on with his fight. The younger poets asked a lot of Williams, but he wanted as much from them, and this relationship, this mutual hankering of the elder poet and a younger poet, is an important facet of the Williams/Norse correspondence. Not only do these letters offer us a glimpse into an individual friendship that has gone almost completely ignored by Williams scholars, but also they may serve as representative letters which throw a little more light on that controversial part of Williams' later years: his influence.

During the ten years (1951-61) that Williams and Norse corresponded, Norse asked Williams to sound out his publishers (James Laughlin of New Directions and David McDowell of Random House and later of McDowell, Obolensky Press) about a manuscript of poems or the Belli sonnets; but Williams approached Norse first, offering to recommend him to McDowell before Norse had ever heard of him and also encouraging Laughlin to publish a book of Norse's poems as early as 1951. All that came of Williams' support, however, was the publication of a single poem,

"The Railroad Yard," in *New Directions 13*. Norse had even less luck with Guggenheim Fellowships for which he asked Williams to write letters of recommendation. One other request that Norse made and Williams enthusiastically granted was a preface to the sonnets of Giuseppe Gioacchino Belli, translated by Norse and published by Jonathan Williams' Jargon Press in 1960. (Williams, for the most part, praised the Belli translations to the skies: "The translations of Belli's sonnets should be read by everyone in America" [see letter of 7 January 1958].) But these were merely favors asked by a lesser-known poet of a well-known poet who had befriended him and who doubtless expected them.

Williams, like Norse, had interest vested in his letters. He was concerned with the survival of his work—not just his own poems, but also the kind of poem that he had largely invented and developed, his tradition, if you like, of non-metrical verse. Norse, Williams felt, would go on with it. Because of the language, the vernacular, in Norse's poems, Williams saw him far out in front of all but a handful of the rest, and this made Williams more than willing to push for Norse "for all that I'm worth." And to push against him when Norse showed him poems in rhyme and meter. In brief, the advice that Norse received was Williams' standard: don't rhyme, eschew meter, abhor inversions, make your lines "more jagged and packed closer with meaning," be American despite America's uncultured ugliness, make every poem recognizably a product of the present day, use the American English that you grew up hearing and speaking, and above all watch out for Eliot! When Norse wrote along these lines, Williams would enthuse; but when he ignored them, he'd get "the cold stuff" back from Williams. Though Norse defended himself at length, sometimes admirably, and struck back on one occasion by attacking *Paterson 5* with hurt reprisals, the result of Williams' criticism was that Norse came back to the "one kind of verse" that interested the master.

After this brief period of disenchantment with Norse's poems, Williams appears to have returned to his initial opinion of Norse as a poet. In his letter of 30 January 1959, he wrote, "Floss read the poems to me and she enjoyed them as much as I did, especially the first, the *Piccolo Paradiso*, that will stand up anywhere among the best poems of our times. . . . You have breached a new lead, shown a new power over the language which makes theories of composition so much blah. . . . Your freedom in the measure is worth all the rest to me." And on 25 April 1960, he told Norse : "It would take at least ten pages to tell you how much I think of you now—my appreciation of the importance of the work you are doing is right in the front of my head." There is no question that Williams, at the end of the correspondence, approved highly enough of Norse to regard him as a leading disciple. Norse, correspondingly, clearly regarded Williams as a great American poet, one of the twentieth-century masters. Even though Williams was no teacher and Norse, it appears in the letters, was more informed about poetic tradition than Williams, there is a master-disciple relationship evident in the letters. When Norse asked Williams time and again to explain what he meant by variable foot, Williams, regardless of the beauty of his poems in this measure (if it is a measure), could be a most frustrating and inarticulate master. Norse never got an answer to his questions and Williams never, anywhere in his writing, made sense of the variable foot (which, truth be told, was a term coined by Edgar Allan Poe to explain how he counted caesurae as feet in a line: the caesura is a variable foot because its measure is determined by the meter of a given poem).

There's every indication in the letters that Williams liked Norse and considered him a friend, and Norse treasured the friendship, doing all he could to restore it when he felt a strain developing. In one letter Williams invited Norse to live at his house in Rutherford to type up the manuscript for his *Selected Essays*. Norse remembers Williams asking him "to move in with them in Rutherford because I cheered Williams up, was young, and he was (as I can experience it now myself) ill and depressed beyond belief. But I declined (much to my regret) as I was afraid the atmosphere would bring me down." Even though Norse left for Italy instead of living with the Williamses in Rutherford, through their correspondence and the frequent visits he made to Williams' house in 1952, 1953 and during the four months of his return visit to New York in 1958, he grew to regard Williams as a close friend. Because of this friendship and the quality of some of Williams' letters to him, Norse was outraged when John C. Thirlwall failed to publish any of the correspondence in *The Selected Letters*, as Thirlwall had promised.

Whatever Thirlwall's reasons for excluding all of the letters to Norse, the correspondence has the value of reflecting Williams' sway, or the nature of it, over writers who emerged in the fifties and sixties. The sympathy, encouragement, warmth, excitement, and hope that Williams expressed in these letters are perhaps not quite what one might have expected. Though it never comes up, Williams probably sympathized with Norse's lack of recognition outside of the little magazines: here, he must have felt, was a young poet fighting against the Establishment and the odds as Williams himself had done.

It's doubtful that the superiority of some of Norse's letters will be enough to draw readers' attention away from the older poet, whose greater gifts and greater importance as a writer are not always reflected in his correspondence. I mean no slight to Harold Norse by this observation—how many poets in the twentieth century are not diminished when placed beside Williams? Over the quarter century since Williams' death, Norse's reputation has grown, internationally, though he still remains less well-known than Ginsberg, Charles Bukowski, William S. Burroughs, and other writers with whom he has been associated. By the time of Williams' death (4 March 1963) or roughly during his first twenty years as a writer, Norse had published three books: *The Undersea Mountain* (Alan Swallow, 1953), *The Dancing Beasts* (Macmillan, 1962) and *The Roman Sonnets of Giuseppe Gioacchino Belli* (Jargon, 1960). Since then he has published eight books of poetry, one of which, *Hotel Nirvana* (City Lights, 1974), was nominated for the National Book Award. His poems were selected with Bukowski's and Philip Lamantia's for *Penguin Modern Poets 13*. Since moving to California in 1968, after more than fifteen years spent in Italy, Greece, Morocco, England, Germany and France (where he supported himself as a teacher and was sponsored by "an Armenian with an Oxford back-ground" who prefers to remain anonymous (see Norse's letter of 29 January 1957), Norse has read his poems with Ginsberg, Burroughs, Bukowski, Ferlinghetti, Robert Duncan, Kay Boyle, Anaïs Nin, Diane di Prima, Michael McClure, Gary Snyder, Philip Whalen, and many others.

He has been allied with the beat poets from nearly the beginning of that movement, and in fact, in William S. Burroughs' words, Norse "played a pivotal role" in "the strange interlude" at the "now-famous Beat Hotel at 9, Rue Gît-le-Coeur in Paris" where the beats stayed from 1958-63. Norse recorded the experience in his Cut-up novella, *Beat Hotel*, first published in Carl Weissner's German translation (Maro Verlag, 1975, now in its ninth printing), in the original English (1983) by Atticus Press, and in Italian (1985) by Stamperia della Frontiera (Norse "was one of the first to apply Cut-ups," says Burroughs, the most famous exponent of the technique, in his preface to the book). Norse has documented this fully in his recently published autobiography, *Memoirs of a Bastard Angel* (William Morrow, 1989), which has greatly enlarged his readership and reputation, with publication in Great Britain (1990) and France (1991). The *Memoirs* were nominated for a Lambda Literary Award.

But Norse is not in any narrow sense a beat poet. Like Bukowski, he has not been assimilable. He had been developing as a poet for more than twenty years before the Beat Hotel became a hospice for the beats; had served as W.H. Auden's part-time secretary during 1939-41; was the close personal friend of Julian Beck and Judith Malina before and during the founding of the Living Theatre; knew E.E. Cummings, James Baldwin, Christopher Isherwood, Anaïs Nin, Paul Goodman, Paul and Jane Bowles, Dylan Thomas, Ned Rorem, Tennessee Williams, Alberto Moravia, Robert Graves, and many other important writers and artists, either before he left for Europe in 1953, or subsequently in Italy, Spain or France. All of these writers have praised Norse and concur in their own ways own ways with Robert Peters who insists that "his work rests firmly on an ongoing tradition of world literature."

As a final note, the lives of these two writers stood in dramatic contrast during the decade of their correspondence. Williams, who had already suffered his first stroke before Norse met him and continued to suffer a series of strokes that over ten years utterly enfeebled him, had all that he could do to keep abreast of the demands that his own creative urges and others placed on him. While Norse published three books, Williams wrote and published fifteen books. While Williams stayed put at 9 Ridge Road, Norse moved from New York to Rome, from Rome to Florence and Naples, travelled through Spain, made a return visit to New York, returned to Italy, moved to France, then Greece, Germany, Switzerland, and London, and moved from place to place within the cities and countries where he lived.

Finally, though Williams suffered severe depression at times because of his strokes, it's hardly apparent in his letters to Norse, which tend to be spirited and supportive. And there's need for him to support Norse, if only because Norse finds so much to complain about. "I certainly seem to be beefing," Norse says in his letter of 26 August 1957, and this is a frequent mood in his letters, a mood not at all unfamiliar to Williams, who complained to his friends for years in his letters that he was being unjustly ignored as a writer — until *Paterson 1* established his place for good.

Of the fifty or more letters that Norse received from Williams, thirty-eight are extant, and there's one letter by Florence Williams dated 16 April 1963, written to Norse one month after her husband's death. These letters, along with the preface to the Belli sonnets and an essay, "The American Idiom", which Williams enclosed with letters to Norse, are held in the Lilly Library, Indiana University, Bloomington. Norse's letters, forty-five in all, are held in The Beinecke Rare Book and Manuscript Library, Yale University. With these letters the Beinecke Library holds twenty-nine of Norse's poems, revisions of poems, and translations of Belli's sonnets, which Norse had enclosed with letters to Williams.

With the exception of Norse's poems, nothing has been cut from the eighty-four letters in the correspondence, the preface to the Belli sonnets, or "The American Idiom". I've made as few editorial insertions as possible, but where I have they are enclosed in brackets, except with regard to the following: Williams' frequent typographical errors and misspellings and Norse's infrequent ones; a few changes in punctuation where these were necessary for the sake of clarity; return addresses for Norse's letters where they've been omitted (all of Williams' letters were written at 9 Ridge Road, Rutherford, New Jersey, his home of fifty years); book titles, which are printed in italics unless the manuscript distinguishes them by capitals; the titles of poems and stories, which are printed within quotation marks. I have not tampered with the poets' inconsistent methods of dating their letters.

I thank Emily Wallace for suggesting this project to me, the University of California at Santa Barbara for a Humanities Research Grant, and Harold Norse for permission to publish his letters and his patient and full responses to my questions.

—John J. Wilson

April 21/75

Dear Howard Nemerov:

I admired your poem "The Painted Yard" for two or three simple reasons. First it was a poem, i.e. it made a thing out of words that said something by the way the words were used. But the thing that struck me most forcibly were the language — it was the language which determined [?] the words were to be used. You worked with the language, [you] your language —

that gather the elements up, letting you made the construction.

If more & the mindless that is forced on us could be forgotten and more that is here to be seen my heart would broaden — welcome life more better. We do not nearly live far & less leave to go before we find good wood. We have tried to start too far up the scale. We have not gone near to the

It is all right to enjoy it but don't (but remember), be run away from the thing where you have to ... ways to some in between ...

water your stock

Sincerely yours

W.C. Williams

saying itself testing it little by little to form.

You have been me free free to go ? for enough and to use the direct way in to ...

I was very moved by ... since which your book ... but it wires be a long turned to get it printed and harder still to sell it. Readers are your ... behind you, very very few know what it is all about

9 Ridge Road
Rutherford, N.J.
April 21, 1951

Dear Harold Norse:

I admired your poem "The Railroad Yard" for two or
three simple reasons: first it was a *poem*, i.e. it MADE a thing
out of words that said something by the way the words
were used. But the thing that struck me most forcibly was
the language. It was the language which determined HOW
the words were to be used. You *worked* with the language,
your language, that *gave* the elements out of which you *made*
the construction.

If more of the instruction that is forced on us could be
forgotten and more that is here to be seen and heard could
possess us — we'd come off much better. We do not realize
how far back we have to go before we find good wood.
We have tried to start too far UP the scale. We have not
gone back to the language itself, letting it dictate its forms.

You have been one of the few to go back far enough
and to use the direct image on its own. I was very moved.
Good luck with your book — but it will be a hard tussle to
get it printed and harder still to sell it. Readers are years
behind you, only a very few know what it is all about.

It is all right to enjoy Eliot but remember, he ran away
from the thing which you have to realize to come out
whole. Watch your step.

Sincerely yours
W.C. Williams

573 Third Ave.
New York, N.Y.
2 July, '51

Dear Dr. Williams,

I returned the latter part of last week & found your letter
waiting, but missed you on two phone calls. I'll try again
next week as I understand you are vacationing.   I hope you
are in good health.   Until next week, then—

Best wishes,
Harold Norse

573 Third Ave.
N.Y. 16, N.Y.
September 22, 1951

Dear Dr. Williams,

I thought you might like to know that the poem you
praised will appear in *New Directions 13*. David McDowell
turned down my volume at Random House, saying
something, by way of explanation, about how R.H.
publishes only the best-known poets and can't afford to
take on unknown ones, etc. T.S. The volume is going to
Farrar, Straus next.

The Becks are getting along with their theatre and I hope it turns out well. Are you starting yr. novel? I'd love to read *The Autobiography*, but I'm in a terrible financial state & can't buy books. Would like to see you again.

Very sincerely,
Harold Norse

9 Ridge Road
Rutherford, N.J.
Sept 26, 1951

Dear Harold Norse:

I wish I could say, Come on out any time, but I'm so damned harrassed with obligations to write or go here or there or just simply to rest or cultivate my wife's company that I can't do it. I never get caught up in my work. Maybe when I get this novel I've contracted to write off my hands, I'll be a man again. I'm not one now, just a machine. I haven't written for pleasure, I haven't written a poem for almost a year it seems. I did write one for the Harvard occasion but I just about sweated my head off to do that. It was no fun.

I'm happy that *New Directions 13* will contain that poem, I'll be looking for a copy of it. It's a good piece of work.

I'll get Random House to send you a copy of *The Autiobiog.* I don't know whether it's good or bad. Non literary people like it, generally speaking. It's a story, that's all, the story of my life. One literary guy snooted it completely, said it was no good. He'd no doubt say the same of my life itself. I don't blame him, I've done my best to lay waste everything he stands for. I hope he breaks his neck.

We'll meet again sometime during the winter. I'm sorry as hell that you're not making out. Anyhow I'll send you the book.

Sincerely
Williams

573 Third Ave.
New York, N.Y.
October 5, 1951

Dear Dr. Williams,

Thanks very much for having Random House send me your *Autobiography*. I'm looking forward to it. I've already heard several people comment on it—they're mostly like the reviewer for whom it was not literary enough, etc., and, like you, I hope they break their necks. I've read *Make Light of It* recently and was bowled over by some of the stories, which I think are little short of amazing. "Danse Pseudomacabre," for some reason, sticks in my crop— probably because I feel it's a prose poem. Others that remain with me: the one about the Jewish couple and the baby; the girl with acne; the baby all out of whack, blue-eyed and relentlessly dying; the German girl who wants to know the *meaning* of America; and many others. I know very well what your work has been adding up to: don't worry, you will be remembered as long as anything remains of this syphilization. I've also been reading much Henry

Miller, recently, and the sheer humor, fecundity, *life* in the man is of heroic proportions. I think there are only two or three great men today in American literature, and you and Miller are certainly there—disliked, maligned by the dandies in a dandy period. I can only hope that eventually, as I live through all the deaths of my own self in this universal death, I will come through, like Lawrence, Miller, yourself, to that realization of the self, that uniqueness and isolation which only a few real *individuals*, those who achieve individuation from the doughy mass of sleepwalkers and goosesteppers, ever achieve.

With sincere gratitude for those four hours at Rutherford and your encouragement,

Harold Norse

9 Ridge Road
Rutherford, N.J.
November 24, 1951

Dear Norse:

Have you tried Ciardi and the Twaine Press? Might be worth looking into.

If you're around in March I want you to read for me on a program for which I'm responsible at the Museum of Modern Art. Lemme know. They've got up a series of poetry readings, several "well known" poets to sponsor 3 unknowns who will read 20 minutes each. The sponsor merely appears, doesn't himself read, merely introduces the others. I don't know the exact date but will let you know later. If you're on the high seas you won't, of course, be able to appear.

Nothing new but the writing on the novel.

Yours
William Carlos Williams

W.C. Williams M.D.
9 Ridge Road
Rutherford, N.J.
12/11/51

Dear Norse:

The date for the reading at the Modern Museum is March 26. Select 20 minutes worth of material—material that it will take you a little less than 20 minutes to read aloud and hold yourself ready to appear at the Modern Museum on that evening.

For myself I wish you'd read the Scranton poem which I first admired. Whatever else you choose will be satisfactory to me.

Best luck
William Carlos Williams

W.C. Williams M.D.
9 Ridge Road
Rutherford, N.J.
December 21, 1951

Dear Norse:

I've sent in your name along with the names of 4 others for the reading March 26 at the Museum of Modern Art. It's quite a crowd but I think that as an introduction it will be better to have a sizable group, to give more men a chance to appear, than to narrow it to 3 as I first intended. Anyhow, that's what we're going to do.

You never gave me the poem by Gascoyne. I'm waiting to see it.

The *Autobiography* isn't selling phenomenally. I understand it'll be about 7000 only by the first of the year. Not even a second edition. I ain't kicking.

You may hear direct from the Modern Museum or you may not. But keep the 26th of next March open.

Best
William Carlos Williams

9 Ridge Road,
Rutherford, N.J.
April 5, 1952

Dear Harold:

I couldn't wangle a grant for you. Of course you've got to have a book. There were many favorable comments on your reading and you'll have one in time.

I know, "in time" is what gets us down but we've got to face it—until we're damned near 70 at times.

Thanks for your letter, I appreciate it. Not that what I

did made much of a splash but it did break the ice. There'll be more such readings and your name will come up again.

As you may have heard I'm going to be at the Library of Congress next year. I don't know what it amounts to but you can count on it, I'll be pushing for you younger men who write as I think one *must* write today for all that I'm worth.

Anyhow, it's April and, damn it, that's always the spring of the year.

Yours
Bill

573 Third Avenue
New York 16,
New York
May 14, 1952

Dear Bill:

Plus ça change! Since my last letter, a few weeks ago, I heard from Alan Swallow, of the Swallow Press, and he has taken my volume for publication! Better late than never.... It's a good thing there are still two or three non-commercial publishers left in these U.S., although from what Swallow writes me, the going is so tough for them, it's a matter of time before they fold up. High costs and no profits.

Waal . . . the date of publication is early spring of 1953 . . . a little less than a year from now. Good time for a small hand-press. I have to cut the book by two-thirds, leaving one-third of the original matter, as Swallow

10

publishes only 48-page first volumes. He can't afford to make them bigger. But for me it's a beginning and I'm glad to accept the chance as such. It won't have as much punch, but it won't be a bad book.

I sure hope I can see you before you travel out to Washington. Have you seen Siegel again? I visited E.E. Cummings first time a couple of weeks ago—one of the most decent, *simpático* people in the world .

My best to Flossie and one of these sunny days let's drink beer on the lawn...

Warmest wishes,
Harold

9 Ridge Rd
Rutherford, N.J.
May 26, 1952

Dear Harold:

You're one of the decentest and most thoughtful guys I know. Oh hell, you know what I mean; no wonder the Commies suppress poems—they're afraid of them, they mean something past ordinary believing. And you make it a personal obligation to keep them clean and EFFECTIVE. I'm glad you're going to have a book even if you have to wait until 1953 for it. Congratulations, I wish you luck with it.

I saw the round-robin of new poems that contained your work and said my say. I don't know whether it has

11

been returned to you as yet. Rhyme is a thing I hate to comment upon—well, see what I have to say. In general you represent the most advanced understanding of the art to be found among that bunch.

We'll get together some afternoon before mid-September, don't worry, and have our beer on the lawn. Meanwhile I've been knocked out by some sort of nervous instability that has me in a bad way, unable to control myself (in my thoughts), depressed, shaky. I believe it's on the way out but until it goes I'm useless to my friends.

Sincerely
Bill

573 Third Avenue
New York 16, New York
June 9, 1952

Dear Bill:

I am very sorry to learn of your illness and hope that by now things are on the upgrade again. No, I haven't yet received the round-robin but looking forward to reading your remarks. I don't employ rhyme so much anymore (I never was addicted to it) but if the emotional force of the poem as I write it demands rhyme, why then I don't fight against it but let it come. As I grow older, I'm much less inclined towards using any rhyme at all—in itself neither bad nor good but depending, I think, upon the honesty and effectiveness of the use to which it is put.

Well, it looks like I might catch a merchantman headed for the North Sea! I will probably get a job on a

Scandinavian ship and leave early in July. But I'll be back around October. Expect to take in London, Paris and, for residence during the summer, somewhere in Italy, not sure where.

I hope you will be feeling well enough to see people in the next few weeks, but if not, we'll table it at your convenience in the fall. Beer on the lawn in the fall—why it's as beautiful as spring! There'll be wonderful colors—and it won't be so damn hot!

The very best of wishes for a good summer!

Sincerely,
Harold

9 Ridge Road
Rutherford, N.J.
Jan. 23, 1953

Dear Harold:

I got a business proposition for you, just thought of it. I need your services as a typist and I need them bad. I've got a chance to sell my prose pieces of criticism, reviews to Random House if I can get them typed. All of a sudden I thought of you. Will you do it for me?

And if you consent the catch is, have you a machine of your own that you can work on at odd hours, etc, etc? I have a machine which is rather broken down but you could live out here and use it if [someone] could take care of your cats. But I imagine you could work better at home—then you can take your own time to [do] it.

It doesn't amount to much—at first. But when you come to copy back the pieces from books it's a horse of another color. But the main thing is to get started on the miscellaneous notes. They will make not more than a book, double spaced, about an inch and a half thick.

Well, there it is. I want it to be a regular business proposition or else nothing doing.

But I'd love to have you do it. Pardon the errors in my typing but with my left hand they are unavoidable.

Best Luck
W.C. Williams

573 Third Avenue
New York 16 New York
May 4, 1953

Dear Bill,

The book is finally out! & here is a copy for you & Florence, with all my best wishes. I spoke to Florence on the phone & she told me you were feeling much better, for which I am very happy. I hope I can come & see you soon, & find out what is happening with you.

I hope my book is not buried or ignored. We shall see. Emanuel Romano has flown to Israel where a museum has been established in his father's name. Romano is a very fine person & I did not know that you were such good friends.

With best wishes,
Harold

9 Ridge Road
Rutherford, N.J.
5/11/53

Dear Harold:

Maybe you have a more intimate name but I don't know it.

Thank you for your book and congratulations on its appearance, the fact that it has appeared, I want to say. I find its interest to be an uneven one and, God damn it, the critics as usual will pick on what they feel to be its weaknesses. This comprises a certain pedestrian tone in what I take to be the earlier poems. A poem must be to some extent unusual in message or form but many of these aren't unusual *enough* so they will escape notice.

But some of the poems are first rate, in fact they are unusually good. Too bad you included the ones which are not standouts. There is always a tendency to include as much as you can in a first book of poems, especially the earlier things to which a man for personal reasons becomes attached.

If you had made a book of such poems as "And All the Travellers Return" I would have gone off the deep end, and I always welcome "Warnings and Promises" whenever I read it. There are several poems of as excellent a quality but somehow the book as a whole needs a good kick in the ass to make it stand up for itself.

This is a hell of a letter to come from me but I see so many books of poems that haven't a thing to recommend them that when I come on the work of a friend in which I believe I want to see him knock 'em dead. Start on the next book right away and make every [poem] in it a standout. Your sentences must be more jagged and packed closer with meaning. Think of their sounds also, the consonants are important.

I like the book, as I say, but as a new offering it isn't unusual enough to attract the kind of attention I think you deserve and should get.

Call up sometime and plan to come out and see me as I have lots of time and as I feel better would enjoy a good talk.

Best luck
Bill

573 Third Avenue
New York 16 New York
May 12, 1953

Dear Bill,

It was very good to hear from you again and to know that you are feeling better. You have REAL friends, you know—and I am one of the realest!

Of course, what you said about the book was honest and that is the most valuable criticism. I'm offering no excuses. All I can say is that the original collection had a lot of poems and some were better, some worse than what finally appeared. But the main objective was to get a book of poems published, for I was getting that submerged underwater feeling, of being NOWHERE, and simply had to take the publisher's taste in *tone*, and Swallow, as you may know, is not a daring man in his selections, but a man of limited taste. That I got a book published at all is the surprising thing.

Now, for the future. Your advice about a second book is splendid. I am working on one—and I doubt whether any publisher will be enterprising enough to publish it. It strikes out into prose poetry and something NEW in poem-poetry, for English, at least. I would like to bring parts of it for you to see. I will be free almost anytime next week except Tuesday night. I'll give you a ring about it. WHAT DO YOU MEAN ABOUT CONSONANTS?

I saw the "Our Lady" poem in POETRY, and liked it fully as much as when you showed me the Ms. It's a tremendous work. A book of such poems would leave no doubt about your stature even in those Eliotic sectors who are so primly, so purely elegant. My God! how you can mix elegance and substance and living, feeling speech!! Dear Bill, you must tell me more about the *technical* matters. Do I let them languish? Jaggedness—that's the thing. In my better moments, I know it—because I write from necessity. And, as you say in PATERSON somewhere, divorce, divorce is the sign of the times! And that business about Hipponax at the end is the key to the thing.

P.S. The Cummingses send their regards.

All my best,
Hipponax

9 Ridge Road,
Rutherford, N.J.
10/26/53

Dear Harold:

When I read your letter (had had your card from France a
month earlier) I could have cheered at your enthusiasm. It
reminded me of my own trip to Italy with my brother in
1909, can you imagine it. The same happened to Goethe
when he wrote of a land where *die citronen bluhn!* In the
gardens of the American Academy in Rome the orange
trees were blooming and the nightingales were singing just
as they were in Boccaccio's day—or in Dante's day also.
Wait till you see Venice! You will not then let yourself
dream any longer.

   But you say you are not talking of such things but of the
Italian people themselves and of Rome! Maybe you have
something there but you'll have to let your eyes open a
little bit at a time—or open all at once to begin with and let
the realization strain itself gradually to the light. It *was* a
great place in the past but to realize it in all its glory you
have to come from a northern and a foggier country where
coal dust clogs the air.

   Don't let anyone however discourage you, the sun in its
brightness is something to behold. Write of the sun even if
it kills you but write with your eyes open and not bemused,
write as it actually is still, no matter what has happened, the
openness with which those Italians embrace it. If you can
do that [bit] hard, hard as they are, you will do an

important piece of work. Make the sun shine again.

It's gonna be a great day! But don't kid yourself, you're gonna have to make yourself (by hand) as innocent as a babe in arms. I'd like to see you attempt it. God bless you.

Here it's coming into November and with what is in the air and in the local political and world situation to say nothing of my own situation, it's nothing to cheer about. I am better and probably will continue to improve but it's slow and will of course be very incomplete. I do as well as I can, as far as I know, and get to New York by bus whenever I have to.

No, I didn't see the reviews of your book except a tiny notice in one of the New York papers which amounted to nothing at all. Very disappointing. Some don't even get that much, keep on plugging. By the way, I like your handwriting, it's legible! I'll put your name up for a grant by the American Institute of Arts and Letters giving them the American Express Co. in Rome address but I don't know whether or not anything will come of it. Do my best.

No use saying, "God bless you," but that's the way I feel nevertheless. Keep your pecker up as me old father used to say.

Bill

Via Dei Foraggi, 74
Rome, Italy
29.12.54

Dear Bill,

I just want to say hello, as it's beginning to look like I'm

settling down here in the "old world", and I may not get out
to Rutherford to say hello in person, which I would like to
do more than you'd suspect. I do not miss the U.S.A. one
tiny little bit. But I do miss certain people—that's all the
States, or any country, for that matter, can ever mean:
people. And you, especially—who had been so kind to me.
I think of you often, out there in that big old house, and I
think of Flossie, and wish I were sitting there with you,
spending many afternoons and evenings. I have just read
The Desert Music two times and I hope you realize how
important a book it is. Of course, you do! All I have to do
is pick up the poetry mags and the little big-selling paper-
backs to know that, outside of a very few who are doing
something new in language and form—that is to say,
having real experiences, not willed ones—much is being
printed that passes for poetry and is actually Ego. *The Desert
Music* is a great book. Remember the night you excitedly
showed me the manuscript of "For Eleanor and Bill
Monahan"? From the opening lines I knew you'd struck
sheer gold. Was that the first of the new form?

Roethke, of course, is a seven-day Wonder! I've never
known him, but would like to. And the young 'uns seem to
be breaking, at last, out of the stiffness of the formal modes
of the forties. At least, in language, if not in actual forms.
Myself, it might please you to know that in the 15 months
I've been in Italy, I've done some 50 poems, half of which
should prove worthwhile. I've even, I think, discovered a
new cadence (I say it tremblingly), which is based on a
mixture of your "musical phrase unit" with accentual prose
stress. We'll see. I call it "phrasal-accentual" verse, and
have invented a little sort of stanza by which I may become
identified. Most of the others I've done have been in a sort

of four-beat line, but the language is original. I shall be sending them out soon, for every little bit of money helps. You know, Bill, that whatever I do in writing is in the teeth of the wolf.

How the hell can I get published in *New World Writing?* They send me polite personal replies saying they are stocked up for a year or two and to send it to them again. But this is maddening. I think that American conveyor-belt efficiency has at last overtaken poetry, the last stronghold. It's good for the poet who gets in, gets known and makes a little money. But like all such business ventures, how much do they give a shit for literature? A lot of deserving people, who are not competitive in psychology (which is one of the things that makes them real artists), are going to get cut out and left on the beach.

I am teaching English to Italians, barely earning a living, but find more time and peace here than in the States. So I think I'll stay as long as I can. I wish I could get hold of your letters for the man who's collecting them, but my mother can't read well now, and they're all in New York.

I would love to hear from you, how you are, how things are financially now. If there's anything I can do for you here at this end, people to see or whatever, let me know. The best of everything to you and Floss for the New Year!

Yours,
Harold

9 Ridge Road
Rutherford, N.J.
1/6/55

Dear Harold:

Glad to hear from ya. May the translation job last
forever or as long as you want it to. You always have been
a light eater as far you have ever told me anything about it.
I shall never cease to regret the time I passed up the
opportunity to give you a meal on that cold night in
Greenwich Village when we had been with my daughter in
law to hear the poet read. When we had recovered our
awareness, it took no more than a moment, you had
evaporated into thin air. In Italy at least you have warmer
weather to breathe.

I had a letter from the Guggenheim people a month or
two back inquiring about you. I gave you the best buildup I
could but knowing so very little about your recent doings I
couldn't be as specific as I should have liked to. Wish you
luck.

It's wonderful to think of you being in Italy, it brings up
so many scenes and things of all that we saw there so
happily. The great baths of Diocletian, for instance, among
the rest. The cathedral at Sienna (tho that I saw on a
previous trip), scenes around Hadrian's Villa at Tivoli and
approaching Amalfi or even Genoa—the railroad station at
night where Floss and I had Caffè Espresso together! It is
very vivid to me as I speak of it. But you have your own
memories which we cannot share. Suffice it to say that it is
all the same Italy which we love, each in his own way, and
so we share it together. It is a magnificent country and a
magnificent region of the world. I don't blame you for
never wanting to leave it.

The only reason for wanting to be in this country is that

for better or worse it does belong to the future. As a poet you will want sooner or later to return to it. There are movements, though not apparent in what we see about us in the colleges which are not alert to them, but moving in the air, in mathematics, in physics, even in medicine, which challenge the intelligence. You are potentially interested in such movements you find in what for want of a better term you must call the New World. It is certainly not the old world that you find in Italy, the Italy of the past which I remember and love.

Well the world moves on to many complex things which in the end turn out to be simple things after all— when we come at last to understand them. For sure we are in a state of confusion now but I am sure we are headed toward the light and the poets, poor bastards, are in the van and will come thru to a simple clarity of approach in the end. But they'd better get over their attempts to obfuscate all about them soon. They can't help it, they are driven by their fates.

Best luck and keep me posted.

Best
Bill

William C. Williams M.D.
9 Ridge Road
Rutherford, N.J.
Nov. 15, '55

Dear Hal:

The translations from the French (possibly the Italian) of G.G. Belli, are superb! both as to the originals and the skill with which they have been rendered into English by you. The effect constitutes a masterpiece. I don't know how I have been permitted by the persons who must know much more of these matters than I do to miss them. It is wonderful of the editors of *Hudson Review* to be so loyal to you under the circumstances. I hope they do not fall by the wayside. Incredible that they have been so harassed by their mere printer in the first place and that they have succeeded in resisting him this far. This translation must not be allowed to die unpublished in English, I sincerely hope that you do not allow this to happen at no matter what sacrifice.

I remember hearing from you just once during the past 6 or 8 months and that letter I answered; with changes of address I am always afraid that letters to friends abroad often go astray.

Pound will be shown your translations at once. When you have completed more of them, send them on. I enclose one buck for the mailing. I wish I could make it more—the second time I have had the opportunity to come to your aid in a small way; this time I don't want to fail again. Wish I could do more.

A new book of poems, *A Journey to Love*, has been published for me by Random House. I'll send you one. These translations have gone to my head, they are so skillfully done and they are so worthwhile in themselves that I can scarcely contain myself.

I keep moderately well and as active as possible under the circumstances. If it were not for Floss, I know, I'd be sunk but since she keeps active I get on. Come again. I won't forget to send the book.

Best
Bill

Via Dei Foraggi, 74
Rome, Italy
20th November, 1955

Dear Bill,

Many thanks for that warm open-hearted praise of my BELLI translations from the ITALIAN—in fact, it is the Roman vernacular in the original, of 125 years ago, so I did it right into familiar American Language. I'll certainly send you more very shortly; I have done about 70 to date. Just received word from HUDSON REVIEW: their contract with old printer, who censored the MS, ends in December, and they promised for SHOOR to print the sonnets in APRIL, 1956 number. That's better than a real long pull. Meanwhile, Jay Laughlin has some others.

If there were one or two others who PRAISE the way you do, there would be one or two other great poets around. Everybody is so cautious nowadays, you'd think they were all born with silver poems up the ass!

I'm very eager to have your new book, *A Journey to Love*, and hope you will write something warm and personal to me inside. Also, I have not got a copy of *Desert Music* and would love to own one. Am poor as a churchmouse but not unhappy and cannot buy books.

Do you think Random House might be interested in doing a complete volume of my Belli translations? Maybe you might interest David McDowell????? Fact is, Belli is the greatest poet in Italy outside of Dante and Leopardi. Has never been translated before into any language at all!!!! I am the only living or dead translator. D.H. Lawrence tried putting him in British North Country dialect. The results were so bad he never published them. Belli was discovered by Gogol, his contemporary whom he most resembles, and both G. and Ste. Beuve wrote essays about him calling him the greatest poet of his time in Italy and one of the world's best of all time. But Belli's work is anti-Catholic, anti-papal, that is; and it uses all the doity woids, so that often he sounds like Henry Miller and Catullus combined. So he is a hard nut for society and publishers to take.

But the time has come....Let me know what Pound says. Or will he write me?? James Joyce admired Belli extravagantly: anyway the writers who really count and don't walk around with hot potatoes in their mouth and pokers up the ass always recognize good work before anyone else climbs onto the bandwagon.

Don't worry, dear Bill, I won't leave any stone unturned to get these translations known. It is only saddening and sickening to know that all the moolah goes to stuffy dull mediocre students and scholars on Fulbrights and Guggenheims, just as it always has: E. Pound said the last word on this in his letters years ago. The scene has not changed. I live on peanuts, which I borrow, while all around me in Rome walk or ride (in long American four-wheeled yachts) the damn stupid Fulbrights, like boy scouts tracking down the dead leaves of scholarship.

Don't break the silence, that's all the guarantors and

chancellors want.

All the best to you and Floss!

Love,
Harold

P.S. I would like to send your letters to the man who requested them from me some time ago. Could you send me his name & address or tell him to get in touch with me? I can arrange for the big batch of them in New York to reach him, too.

Thanks for the buck. But please don't send any money unless you can *really* afford to.

9 Ridge Road
Rutherford, N.J.
Nov. 26, '55

Dear Hal:

I sent your letter together with your translations from Belli at once to Pound—but he spoke slightingly of the man and of your translations, that they were not rhymed, etc, etc, but don't let that bother you. He never acknowledges anything as good unless he, *der grosser Ich*, has had a hand in bringing it to the world's attention. I have been frequently nauseated at his pretensions but there are extenuating circumstances which make me stick to him, God damn him to hell.

All you can send me of the translations the more I will

be pleased. Gogol's name is enough for me as one of his backers. The colloquial English or more properly American you are using in your work is the precise thing that makes it possible. And that is something you know well, none better. In fact what attracted me most to what you were putting down was the language you were using. I was thrilled at it, it gave me that feeling of *le mot juste* which penetrated to the tips of my toes. The handling of that language makes a masterpiece of what you are doing and don't let anybody tell you different.

It is good news that *Hudson Review* is not going back on you. April is not too far off but we can afford to wait. Aye, aye! to all you say of the Fulbright boys and girls, I suspect, but I have not had the opportunity that you have had to observe them. You are going it on your own, more power to you though it must at times be hard. There's no substitute for being up against it for your very food and lodging to make for a sense of the real in all you touch.

I have ordered some more copies of *Journey to Love*. As soon as they arrive I'll send it on to you together with *Desert Music* and another book, *The Dog & the Fever*—a translation from the Spanish. Hope you like 'em.

You can't imagine how you have ripened during the last year and how happy I am to see it—though it may have cost you many pangs of disappointment and loneliness to have come on this far. I do you homage as a friend of whom I am inordinately proud.

Sincerely
Bill

If Laughlin already has some of the Belli translations I'd

better be on my guard about speaking to Random House about them officially. At the same time since I see Dave McDowell almost every week I'll speak to him to sound him out on the possibility of Random House doing a complete book of the Belli translations. It should be a hit with the present temper of the world. No wonder Lawrence didn't go on with the work: he didn't know enough of the language it requires to make it convincing.

O.K. about the buck.

I'll speak to Thirlwall about the letters, you'll hear from him when he gets round to it.

Best.

Via Dei Foraggi, 74
Rome, Italy
8 Dec., 55

Dear Bill,

Thanks again for the enthusiastic support. Nothing helps more. Re Pound: *der grosser Ich* is indeed its own limitation. It is precisely that which keeps him from greatness—in another age, the Renaissance and, perhaps, Roman times, it was possible to have it and be great. But today, it is a disease, an affair of the nerves. If I had been able to respect it in poets of big reputations, to flatter and please, I should have been granted *favors* from these lordly personages. Auden, for instance, was a friend, but when it became apparent that I would not submit to kissing the hand and obeying orders, he ceased to regard me as such.

29

Pound is certainly the most important critical figure in twentieth-century letters, no one has done more to bring it about. He LOOMS—and you can't take that away from him. But two things he lacks: experience of life and the mystic sense, by which I mean, recognition of forces greater than the self. It is ironic that his own chief literary idols possessed BOTH of these characteristics in abundance, plus that knowledge of craft in which Old Ez shines *today*, vide Villon, Dante, Li Po, Catullus, etc. Yes, even Catullus, for all his ego, conveyed real humility and a sense of the existence of the gods. AND THE JAPANESE NOH, purely mystic!

Now, Pound has discovered and midwifed first-rate stuff. But he has also been way out on a limb, in many cases, especially where, as you say, he hasn't had a hand in it. He saw Auden, at the start, as another Flecker, small stuff; he didn't recognize Dylan Thomas, he under-rated D.H. Lawrence—in summa, anything that wasn't *in his line* he couldn't see. Also, he pushed Antheil like a real god of music; and Antheil always was second-rate, from the start, and ended up in Hollywood, nothing a real composer would have touched with a pole. Also Bunting, second-rate. And others. His anti-semitism reveals that all the despised middle-west narrow provincialism against which he fought in literature had never entirely left his own psychology. He could write the *ABC of Reading*, but he had never learned the ABC of Being. But let's not hold that against him. I admire him, all the same, for what he *has* done; what he *hasn't* is what makes him human. I'm sorry he didn't take to the Belli translations, nor to Belli himself. And one can always learn from him. Is he, by the way, just cantankerous, as at the start, or did he really develop some sort of psychosis during his Fascist days? Nobody is wholly sane today, anyway, how can he be??!

Well, you are the only leading poet who has been a *good friend*. Tate is very kind, and supports the translations; Cummings has offered recommendations for a Guggenheim, with the warning that his is like the kiss of death to such committees; Shapiro has offered a rec., too. But *you!!* My God, how it helps to know you are *with* one, and your *human* touch, above all!!! It is precisely all those years of delivering babies and forcing open the wombs of the poor, fighting little girls with diphtheria, etc., that have given you the experience, aside from the talent, which makes your prose and poetry unique. Your chances of survival are better than most; in poetry, if not criticism, better even than Pound's.

Well, I have learned just about everything poverty has had to teach, after a lifetime in *that* school. Now I've reached the point where remaining broke can only do more harm than good. What I need most is LEISURE to produce. In fact, the Belli translations were done after someone I know had patronized me for several months, and I had the freedom to do uninterrupted work. Otherwise it would never have been done.

Yes, the loneliness and the disappointment—they're not over. But I've got hope, at the bottom of old Pandora's box. My battle now is to get subsidized so that I can concentrate on turning out worthwhile stuff. All the gravy still goes, as always, to the lily-white scholars, most of whom don't even *need* grants. Creative effort is like the red flag in the Pentagon. Committees blanch when they see it. Although I ain't a communist, and never will be, as I detest ALL political parties, I might as well be one as be a poet. They seem to mean the same thing to the universities and the foundations.

Bill, you are PERFECTLY FREE to mention OFFICIAL-LY to David McDowell that the Belli is on sale, if Random House will take it!! I've sent a group to Laughlin ONLY for the annual anthology, *not* to be considered for a book, and he has no rights whatsoever as yet, as I haven't even heard from him about the annual. So, more power to you! The only hitch is, some of the best of the translations are, from the censor's viewpoint, obscene. But all the same, let's see what we can do. I'm sending you, under separate cover, *sans* letter, for it is cheaper that way, another batch of the Belli. Will mail it in a few days. It would make a good seller, as a matter of fact; the poems are funny, narrative, and as "dirty" as Henry Miller or Joyce (who admired B. enormously).

I've sent some of your letters to Thirlwall from here, and given him my poor ole mother's address in New York, where he can pick up the others.

Am eagerly awaiting arrival of your books. Can't thank you enough. Hope you write something for me on the front page. You're the only friend I've asked that of—I never even asked Dylan, who was a good friend, to do that. I only want it when it *means* something and the writer *means* it, and from you that's the way it is!!!

My very best to Floss, take good care of yourself, and I know that Floss will keep things going.

With warmest affection,
Harold

Pardon the LENGTH of this! And SEASON'S GREETINGS!!

9 Ridge Road,
Rutherford, N.J.
Dec. 14/55

Dear Hal:

I've waited 3 weeks for Random House to send me my own books from no further away than New York City! This morning I called up their office and got only an office girl who assured me that there had been some mistake, etc, etc, and that I would receive the books at once! I'm looking just above my desk at one of my favorite pictures, a snapshot of a snowy cornfield whose trees, in the background, are glittering with ice; maybe you'll receive the books before that ice melts. In fact I hope to get the books off to you by this weekend.

Don't mind Pound, in many ways he's just a baby, has never grown up. You're right, his mid-western heritage still has him ice-bound like the trees in the picture of which I was just talking. In spite of that he's the most informed literary man of our era. God help us, then.

I'll speak to Thirlwall of the letters. Very good of you to take the trouble. I'll also talk to McDowell about the Belli translations but don't know what Random House will do about it. Maybe they'll be willing to look them over— I'll do my best. You should hear from Dave McDowell in the course of the next few weeks direct. Best luck .

I'll inscribe the books appropriately, never fear. I feel honored that you ask me to do it.

This letter must be got off at once so I won't drag it out unduly. I'm now getting myself ready for a reading of my poems at Wellesley College on Jan.16, quite a job for me

now. That takes up the time when I'm not working on a
short story, a long short story, of 50 or more pages. No
guarantee that it will be any good but, as usual, it will be
along a new line. Maybe I'll send you a copy of it in about
2 months when I pray and hope it will he finished.

Hope the books reach you in good order.

Best
Bill

Via Dei Foraggi 74
Rome, Italy
Feb 9, 1956

Dear Bill,

Sunny Italy is cold as the hinges of hell. And naturally
since the Romans never admit it gets cold in Rome, there
are rarely decent heating arrangements and I'm sitting here
typing this with numb fingers. I haven't removed my socks
for a week for fear of frostbite. The whole Mediterranean
area is unnaturally arctic and an icy wind from Siberia has
been blowing steadily for ten days. The papers say it won't
let up for another week.

Hope things are warmer in Rutherford.

Now I want to ask you if you could write a preface to
my Belli translations for a book of them that is being
planned here. Alberto Moravia, the famous Italian novelist,
has already given me an introduction he wrote, which will
be used along with yours, as he is no judge of the English
translations; but his introduction serves to introduce the

reader to the greatness and importance of Belli in world literature, and yours would treat of the literary value of my translations as English poems. It would be of inestimable assistance if you could do this. It needn't be too long—a couple of pages of what these translations mean to you and what importance they have as poems, their use of language, etc. Please let me know if and when I can expect your preface. Also, do you know whether Laughlin or McDowell can do anything by way of taking copies for American distribution under their imprint?

I just sent you a letter last week thanking you for the three books and your dedications, so I haven't much more to add in this one, except that beyond any doubt whatsoever, those last two books of poems stand as great works in our time, or any time.
Ciao! Best to you and Floss!!

Harold

William C. Williams M.D.
9 Ridge Road
Rutherford, N.J.
Feb. 15/56

Dear Harold:

Consider the thing done. I'll write the 2 or 3 pages of the Belli introduction before the end of the month. It will be wise to have Alberto Moravia write the historical and biographical note for I of course know nothing more of the man than the present work and what you have told me in your letters. My job will be only to speak, only, of the translation. That, I can see, is developing into quite a job.

I'll show your letter to Dave McDowell and ask him if Random House is interested in your proposition then, if we can't do business with him, to Jim Laughlin. You'll hear from me later on these scores. Thirlwall went to see your mother I think—but you must know more about this than I do by this time.

I was out reading my verses to an audience in Newark last night, a straight commercial engagement to advertise a brand of pianos. It was a small audience made up I suspect mainly of teachers from a nearby normal school. They were friendly enough but totally uninformed on what I was talking about. It is tiring to me to feel that I am talking against such a front. I felt entirely off my base. I realize at such times how far an American audience has to go before it can even listen intelligently to anything concerning a theory of what is going on in my world. I feel like a stranger. No doubt that is the way they think of me, a wild man who is totally incomprehensible.

You'll hear from me again, right now I feel too weary to continue. You are getting winter while here it is warm. Such is climate.

Keep working.

Yours
Bill

9 Ridge Road
Rutherford, N.J.
Feb. 29/56

Dear Hal:

Here it is, I hope you can use it. I spoke to McDowell
about detailing the book, about Random House detailing
the book, but he didn't think they'd want to do it. I haven't
spoken to Jim Laughlin as yet but I will do so as soon as I
see him.

Flossie objects to my "ass from their elbows" bit* but
rather than remove it I leave that to you if you want to, I
won't object.

Hope the weather in your part of the world is
moderating a bit—as of course it must soon do. It has been
a pleasure to write this for you on a work which fascinates
me. Good luck with it and be sure when it is printed to
send me a copy. Wish I could flip myself over there to
have such a man as you to take me round the town. I saw
Rome with my brother 60 years ago and later with Floss
and often think of those days with intense longing.

Sincerely
Bill

I've made no copy of this piece so sit right down and
copy it if you want to preserve it. W.
*I object because I think it detracts from Belli's
statements. All the rough stuff should come from Belli!
[Added by Mrs. Williams]

[enclosure: Feb. 29, 1956]

THE SONNETS OF GIUSEPPE GIOACCHINO BELLI TRANSLATED INTO THE AMERICAN IDIOM BY HAROLD NORSE

Gorki wanted to do the job and D.H. Lawrence and Joyce each into his own language but they were written not in the classic language, Italian, that scholars were familiar with, but a Roman dialect which gave them an intimate tang that was their major charm and which the illustrious names mentioned above could not equal. The idiom that they most affected was a language of the people to whom the sonnets were addressed and for whom they were written. Without a change of heart among scholars they would be rebuffed by such an attitude of mind as was Belli's. The nature of the shocking facts he had to disclose with such ironic candor in such a form as the sonnet, of all forms, so used to being employed for delicate nuances of sound and sense, forbade in their minds cruder employment.

But that is just the point which insists on being made. The times were crude, especially so for the underdog of whom these sonnets deal, but not so crude that they could not see themselves, in their imaginations, in high office. Belli saw it also and he knew how, politely, to bring them down and up! to their betters by a knowledge of the language.

What could a Joyce or a Lawrence do with such material or probably a Gorki either? It was a perfect situation for exploitation by an idiom which had no classic pretentions, in fact rebelled against all scholarship, yet held its head high. What could be better than an idiom of one of the greatest countries of the world that as yet had no official standing, the American? This would be the language to use for the translation, a language comparable to the original Roman dialect.

And what was more appropriate to this purpose than an American conversant with this idiom by long acquaintance with it, from childhood, now living in Rome, an informed poet, a poet living very often a hand to mouth existence for his craft? He knows what Belli had the heart to feel for his fellow Romans of the period in which he lived.

The idiom into which Harold Norse has translated these sonnets was inaccessible to anyone before the present time. American scholarship doesn't know its ass from its elbow as far as the resources of this idiom are concerned for [scholars] have had only the "English" of their bringing up dinned into their ears until they have grown insensitive to everything else about them. It is not only the words which should be noted but the way in which they are spoken which characterizes this idiom. Harold Norse knows this medium, knows moreover its dignity, and has a deep love for it, for it is his own.

Not to want to appear cryptic, it is necessary to push the point a little further: these translations are made not into English but into the American idiom in which they appear in the same relationship facing English as the original Roman dialect does to classic Italian. The idiom spoken in America is not taught in our schools but is the property of men and women, which though they do not know it, is one of the greatest of modern languages waiting only for a genius of its intrinsic poetry to appear.

The difference between it and the language taught to us in our schools is essentially a prosodic one which we have only as yet recognized by ear. The measure is what we refuse to recognize, the "metre" as Chaucer calls it in his poem in which he speaks of Boethius. It is in the measure of our speech, in its prosody, that our idiom is distinctive. That Harold Norse has as birthright, which makes him at home with this translation.

He has succeeded with it in producing felicitous lines when anyone not so equipped inevitably must have failed. It has waited until the present to have these fascinating and shocking and irreverent sonnets of Belli to come to the eyes of the English speaking world. Sometimes there appears to be a justice in literary history.

William Carlos Williams

Via Dei Foraggi, 74
Rome, Italy
12 March, 1956

Dear Bill,

Many thanks for the Preface to the Belli translations. I would have answered sooner but I was seriously ill & weathered the worst without a doctor or medicine or food. But when I began spitting & coughing blood, a doctor was sent for by friends & he said I had just pulled through pneumonia in a remarkable fashion & that I had the constitutional strength of 3 men & that now I was very

12 March, 1956

Dear Bill,

Many thanks for the Preface to the Belli translations. I would have answered sooner but I was seriously ill & weathered the worst without a doctor or medicine or food. But when I began spitting & coughing blood, a doctor was sent for by friends & he said I had just pulled through pneumonia in a remarkable fashion & that I had the constitutional strength of 3 men & that now I was very weak. So I've been in the house convalescing for almost 2 weeks. Please — not a word to Thirlwall as he may see my mother again & I don't want her to know anything about it under any circumstances. The worst is over, I'm recuperating, & if she knows anything, it'll kill her!   (over)

2

Bill, some questions about the "Preface":

1) You start by saying " Gorki wanted to do
the job and D.H. Lawrence & Joyce...." but
only Lawrence tried, as far as we know, to
translate B. Gorki never enters the picture —
it was Gogol who discovered but did not
try to translate him. & Joyce who admired
him. How to change this paragraph???
Shall I send it to you & have you
change it ??

2) what is the word after "fascinating" in
the last sentence?: " It has waited
until the present to have these fascinating
and sh ching and inaverent
sonnets of Belli to come to the ages of
the English speaking world. "

I've just corrected the proofs of the Belli
for Hudson Review so it should
be out next month! Hooray!!

        Will write again soon. Let me
        know about above.
                                    Best,
I think Flossie is right about   Harold
their "ass from their elbows".

weak. So I've been in the house convalescing for almost 2 weeks. Please—*not a word to Thirlwall* as he may see my mother again & I don't want her to know anything about it under any circumstances. The worst is over, I'm recuperating, & if she knows anything, it'll kill her!

Bill, some questions about the "Preface": (1) You start by saying "Gorki wanted to do the job and D.H. Lawrence & Joyce..." but *only* Lawrence tried, as far as we know, to translate B. Gorki never enters the picture—it was Gogol who discovered but did not try to translate him. How to change this paragraph??? Shall I send it to you and have you change it???

(2) What is the word after "fascinating" in the last sentence? "It has waited until the present to have these fascinating and sh ching and irreverent sonnets of Belli to come to the eyes of the English speaking world."

I've just corrected the proofs of the Belli for *Hudson Review* so it should be out next month! Hooray!!

Will write again soon. Let me know about above.

Best,
Harold

I think Flossie is right about their "ass from their elbows."

9 Ridge Road,
Rutherford, N.J.
Mar. 16/56

Dear Hal:

You must have the constitution of an ox—but I'm glad you got a doctor at last. You must have been mighty sick. Thank goodness you came through. Do you need a small loan? Say fifty dollars, I'd be happy to send it to you—it may tide you through a crisis. Be sure your mother will not hear of what you have been through from me.

The word you couldn't make out is "shocking". Leave out the reference to "ass from their elbow"; fill in the space with something appropriate. I agree with Floss's dictum.

I am sorry I mixed up the reference to Gogol. Go over what I said about Lawrence and Joyce and correct it, writing in the truth of whatever happened. There is no need to return the article to me, I trust you completely to correct the text yourself—just send me a copy of what you did.

Don't hesitate to ask me for the five grand, I can afford it and you don't have to return it ever if you want it—I suppose I should send it at once without waiting to hear from you but I'm not in the habit of doing that sort of thing.

At the present moment it's hailing, I think, after snowing heavily all morning, the heaviest snowfall of the winter. Pardon me, but it's marvellous to me! I only wish it had [kept up] and will go on all night. It quiets the nerves. If it had not occurred I would have felt that the whole winter would have been lost, spring would have been an anti-climax.

Oh, I forgot to say that it is good news that the *Hudson Review* is printing the Belli translations. I'll have to subscribe, they published a snide reference to me some years back and I've been off them since then. But I don't want to miss your translations.

Take care of yourself. The Italian spring can be marvellously beautiful and when one is convalescent from a severe illness it is one of the chosen moments from which to witness it. Best luck from us both, Floss sends her love.

Bill

Via Dei Foraggi, 74
Rome, Italy
29.3.56

Dear Bill,

Thanks very much for the offer of 50 dollars, but really, although I am pretty broke, what with assistance from those who can spare it without feeling it, I am able to tide over this period. I wouldn't want to accept financial assistance from you anyway, who have helped me and wished me well in so many ways. It's a good thing I have found people here, rich people, who still care enough about poetry to want to help out poets. So forget about the money, and God bless you for the offer!

I'm still weak as a kitten, so I haven't gotten around yet to fixing up the few details of fact in your introduction, but when I do, any day now, I'll send you a copy, as you requested.

As for the 'udson Review, you ain't the only one who got bopped by 'em. My only previous encounter with them was when one of the editors, Arrowsmith, reviewed my book, *The Undersea Mountain*, and got pretty nasty about it. Still, it was reviewed with Dylan Thomas' *Collected*, and

MacNeice and Edwin Muir, Jean Garrigue and one or two others of that sort, so I guess after all they considered it a not insignificant first volume, and also praised, before damning the rest, my ability to handle the craft of verse. So now I make a pretty strong appearance in its pages, the very same editors are bending backwards to praise my work in the Belli. So, as with most mags, I wouldn't pay any attention to their jibes or indifference. If you've got something, sooner or later they come around and acknowledge it.

Spring has only just begun here, with one or two splendid days. The oleanders and almonds are blooming, the tourists are beginning to pour in from all over the world, swarming with cameras and odd forms of dress. Rome is a warm and languid metropolis, when it is not having freak snows and northern cold, which happens once every millennium. I'm writing poetry in Italian! Some of it is better than my Amurrikun verse, I think, and I will translate it myself. It's a new gimmick, but then I'm liable to do anything. My chief problem in English is how to overcome the formalistic elements and strike the individual note that comes when I let my language take care of itself. I've never had anyone tell me much about writing, you see, and jes grew, like Topsy, as a poet. For better or worse, I absorbed a lot from the teachings of Tate and the New Critics—but not, as some critics have said I did, directly, as I never read those boys. I jes absorbed it out of the air, and had the misfortune to go to college. Mostly, I grew up on Hart Crane, my only influence, although my recent work shows none of it. What the hell! Why doesn't someone tell me something about poetry??!!? I wish you would answer one question:

IN YOUR INTRODUCTION TO MY BELLI YOU STATE THAT SOMEONE COULD COME ALONG AND USE THE RICH COLLOQUIAL AMERICAN TONGUE THAT IS JUST WAITING TO BE USED AND IMMORTALIZED IN POETRY—DO YOU THINK MY TRANSLATIONS ARE A BEGINNING IN THAT DIRECTION?? *AND, SHOULD I DO IT IN ORIGINAL VERSE???????*

This is very serious. If I make that step, and I have, as you say, the background for it, it means chucking overboard the whole traditional language I grew up on. Yet, under that traditional language is the bedrock, the mother tongue of Brooklyn, USA, that I heard my momma and dad battle in, and they fought! And their diction was not what I subsequently heard from lecture platforms at college. They were not squeamish, in those daily fights, about their language. My biggest shame, as a boy, was to be with a group of friends outside the house we lived in, and to hear the raised voices of my progenitors ripping off choice gutter-expressions, much to the delight of my comrades; and the painful shame I experienced made me vow two things: (a) never to marry, and (b) to escape from that shame into becoming a great writer. The first I have, unfortunately, observed. The second, and I am not getting any younger, is a tougher battle than I thought. Still, I've got something, and it's got to come out better than it has. Can you say anything that will straighten me out? Once, some six years ago, you started our friendship by singling out my poem, "Warnings and Promises," from a group, and giving it high praise, chiefly for the language employed. Since then, I have not especially used or written in that language, although your opinion about it I have always valued. It's just that, I don't know what my individual voice is, or how to develop it.

Well, these are big demands. Still, you are one of the handful of living people, maybe two or three, who is able to see above the mud-line of modern verse. So I'll value anything you say. Keep well and

Love to you and Floss,

Harold

William C. Williams, M.D.
9 Ridge Road
Rutherford, N.J.
April 21/56

Dear Hal:

This'll be a brief letter for I have only one thing to say in it: the American idiom is your native language, if you abandon it in favor of standard English you have lost your major opportunity to face the future of an expanding prosody. It's up to you. What you remember of your parents' speech when roused may have been vulgar but it contained a priceless element of verbal organization; its metrical arrangement. If you can make lines which embody that you will have created a new mode of speech, as new to the world and as welcome as Einstein's law of relativity.

Glad you're over the pneumonia and hope you'll soon be on your feet again, Italy in the springtime is fabulously beautiful! Make the most of it. It's good news that the

Hudson Review is sticking by you. I'll be looking forward to the appearance of the first of the Belli translations, don't overload them with marginalia, what cannot be understood at sight is often best omitted.

We've just been on a poetry reading trip to Puerto Rico. It was delightfully sunny and warm there, now we're freezing again. The sun is the source of light but also of poetry though darkness is pregnant more often than not with poetry.

Sincerely yours
Bill

Presso Kimball
Via Santo Spirito 32
Florence, Italy
[undated]

Dear Bill,

I have had no certain address for a while, so I haven't written sooner, but from now on, whether I am staying at the above address or not, any mail sent to me there will get to me.

Right now I am in Florence, taking it easy, as I am still weak from that bout with pneumonia, and slowly convalescing. It is a wonderful city to convalesce in *albeit* I am looking over my typewriter into a dreary fall of rain and the day is gray. But it is Florence, and it is Spring! I don't get around much, so as not to weaken myself, but sometimes I stand on the Ponte alla Carraia, which is just

near the house where I am staying with a friend, and at
dusk the whole city seems to pass over the bridge. And in
this way, more than looking at the paintings and frescoes
and statues, all of which I have seen anyway, I feel that I am
traveling, seeing the city, getting around. I may be able to
rest up this summer and so regain my strength, for at last it
seems slowly to be flowing back, thank God!

Have you seen the HUDSON with my Belli
translations? Evidently, they are making reprints of them,
for they deducted about 60 bucks from my check, without
consulting me, but I suppose it's all to the good. In the
meanwhile, the publisher who was going to bring out the
book has gotten cold feet—afraid of possible censorship in
England and America, with consequent loss of money. So I
don't know what will happen as far as publication in book
form is concerned.

Meanwhile, I keep seeing the little Fulbrights, like spots
before my eyes, upon whom America lavishes so much
money for dubious scholarly pursuits. An entire fortune is
being spent on them—and a deader, less imaginative, more
reactionless group of cephalopods would be hard to find.
How do you suppose I must feel, who have never received a
grant of any kind, when those blithering boobs gather
around me like flies around honey, having read my work,
laughed at my jokes, *learned*, by Jesus! yes, learned, from me!!
And then, the inevitable: Are you here on a Fulbright? And
I must answer in the negative. What kind of a country do
we come from that supports plodders in style and lets its
talent go to the dogs? "What do you do on your Fulbright?"
Reply: "Just fuck. There's a nice German girl I'm keeping
on it, if you must know." This was a more cynical, more
dissatisfied type than most.   Please let me know how things

are and what's new. When are the *Letters* being published?
All the best to you and Floss,

Warmly,
Harold

Via Santo Spirito 32
Presso Kimball
Florence, Italy
August 21st, 1956

Dear Bill,

I hope all is well for you, as I have not heard from you
for some time. I believe I sent two letters, and I hope, if
you have replied, that your letters have not gone astray, as
they sometimes do in this disorganized country.

Have you seen the Belli translations in HUDSON? I
have not heard, so far, of any reactions, favorable or
otherwise, and I wonder how they have been received. No
angry letters of protest, no noisy condemnations, no
praise—nothing. Just complete silence so far, unless the
editors have seen fit to keep such responses to themselves
and me in the dark. Henry Rago has taken a very long
poem of mine for POETRY, called 'Florence', but I don't
know when it will appear. Also, some prose pieces from a
travel book on Italy that I have been writing every now and
then—they should appear in POETRY around Christmas,
he says.

What has been happening to your forthcoming book of
letters? No word from Thirlwall. Is he using my piece

about our first meeting? I hope you both liked it.

The heat here is pretty awful, but I'm glad I'm here, just the same. I wish you'd write and let me know how you and Floss are and what's new. I've just been reading that ass Oscar Williams' *Pocket Anthlology of American Verse*—the man's taste is all in his pocket. He's an advertising man gone astray into the field of poetry. What real poet would give so false a representation of what pretends to be "500 American Masterpieces"? 14 pp. of Emily Dickinson, 11 pp. of Cummings, 6 pp. of W.C. Williams (!), 8 pp. of Robert Lowell, 18 pp. of Ezra Pound, 5 1/2 pp. of Karl Shapiro— and 19 pp. of Oscar's wife, Gene Derwood!! And 16 pp. of himself!!! And the omissions! Jean Garrigue, Joan Murray, Randall Jarrell, James Agee, W.T. Scott, and how many more. Such humility. Such taste.

Do let me hear from you. All the best for a cool and productive summer.

Affectionately,
Harold

9 Ridge Road
Rutherford, N.J.
August 27/56

Dear Hal:

We've spent all summer on the home lot and a very comfortable summer it's been all in all though rather chilly during July. Everything if you'll remember stops dead literarywise during the summer, that is all to the good from my present viewpoint. I'm surprised that you have received no letters from me since I have certainly written you since the Belli publication. Morgan of *Hudson Review* sent me the issue and a good letter speaking of it. Historically the translations were very interesting and needed to be done and published—but the sonnet form without the complex rhyme schemes of a sonnet being carried out in minute detail leaves something to he desired. No one is shocked by revelations as to the Pope's household, all they say is, of course, what do you expect? I haven't heard any word either.

I'm glad POETRY is publishing you this winter, you need a cumulation of such publications for your next book, to put it across.

The letters, as far as I know, are going forward normally tho' I suspect that Thirlwall is a little sore at me—and I don't blame him too much. The thing is (and this modifies what I said earlier about things letting down literarywise in summer) a woman professor at Fairleigh Dickinson *University!* (things happen fast in this neck of the woods) has been engaged this spring and summer in writing a master's thesis on me. She has been coming in to see me once or twice every week to take down what I have to say about myself. I did not tell Thirlwall anything about it until quite recently—why should I have done so, it was a private matter and I was very careful to forewarn him when he began with me that I would not give him a contract. So that if he is sore and has lost interest in the letters that will be just too bad, the world has withstood greater shocks than its possible failure to see my letters at all.

As far as that shit O.W. is concerned, forget it. I am amazed at such a house as Scriblers [sic] for letting themselves in for such a cheap bastard—the only thing I will say for myself is that I had the acumen to see through him at the first. How a person could be so blind to accept the things he does as feats of common honesty is beyond me. I wouldn't give one of his vile anthologies houseroom. Out with them. I will say for Scribners that recently, I have heard, they have thrown him out, the slimy cocksucker.

With that sweet goodnight (rhetorical, for it is almost noon) I will bid you adieu, these are foul times we live in but in any age possibly the rats will always creep in—possibly it was no different in Athens and Rome. I have been reading the poems of Horace as translated 30 years ago by Horace Gregory, and they are filled with laughing invective, I strongly recommend the book—it is one of the most refreshing in its candor, entirely unconscious, that I have ever read.

Toor-a-loo
Bill

Florence
21/8/56
[Sept. 21]

Dear Bill,

Just got back from a month at the seashore, a small port on the Tyrrhenian coast called Porto Santo Stefano, with the typical mixed modern houses mingling up into the hills with Moorish façades and just plain rubble and ruins, and found your letter waiting for me in Florence. I'm not as strong as I was, thanks to the virus pneumonia that I fought without benefit of wonder drugs or clergy last February in Rome, and even now have periods when it looks as if any extra physical effort will produce a relapse; so here am I, a convalescent and semi-invalid, picking my way through the vast pleasure-peninsula that is Italy, and through poetry and sniffs of death at my tender age, which is not so tender after all. How I do it, God only knows! But it is wonderful to see the sun here, to feel the old Italian warmth, mindless and sensual, seeping through the skin, and to hear the bold virile Italian language all around me, sung, shouted, laughed. But never mumbled, never whispered nor apologetic. It gives life. But, at times, and I do not tell this to everyone, I have sneaking little hankerings for the ugly old city I grew up in, hideous New York with its neurotics and apologies and self-justifications, on which a whole country, a whole society is built. Not to stay in—never that, my Gawd!—but to visit, to palp gingerly with the fingertips, like a blind man reading Braille—and then to flee from. I have never been so unhappy as in New York, and to think I spent practically my whole life there! If I had to return to the States, I'd set myself up in San Francisco or its environs. It seems the only human place, as I remember it, in the whole length and breadth of the country, with possible exceptions, such as New Mexico, Arizona and other western reservations, although they blow up H-Bombs around there.

I was a little disconcerted by your remarks about the Belli translations. I hope you are not experiencing a change of heart about them, but you do sound a little like nasty old Uncle Ezra when you say "... the sonnet form without the complex rhyme schemes of a sonnet being carried out in minute detail leaves something to be desired"—are you reneging on the excitement you felt when you first read them and danced on the tips of your toes with joy because of the *language*?!? I certainly agree that rhyme is essential to sonnets (I actually do rhyme carefully in a large number of them), but don't you think, as you have written in previous letters, that the language and sheer verve of these carry them off and make them more than just "historically... interesting" as you write in this last letter? Well, sometimes it is all very discouraging. Morgan, who seemed just as enthusiastic as you were when he accepted them and wrote me dozens of praiseworthy letters, now that they have been published in HUDSON, writes me very casually, does not send me news of who said what about them, merely that reactions were mixed, some thought them "very good and others very bad". It is hard to know what people think, especially when they themselves (or we ourselves) are subject to change, like everything else, and are never in one position about anything very long.

But that's the way of the world, our human condition, and fuck it, we are all like that, even when we don't think we are, and we have to accept it and live with it. The important thing is not to be a snake like that shitass O.W. Those initials stand for the sound one makes when one picks up a "poem" or an anthology of his. The moment I laid eyes on the creature, ten or eleven years ago, I thought of "spider", "hunchback", "toad". And I was not wrong. If a spider could talk, it would be just the kind of voice he has—and would say the same things. But let's forget that. It brings no credit upon one to crush a spider, and anyway, in this case, we can't. They hold all the key positions of power, the insects and rats.

I'm sorry to hear about the tiff with Thirlwall. I think he'll go ahead with the Letters anyway, why should't he? Of course, not having a contract makes him feel a trifle insecure, no doubt. Still, why should the fact that a female professor from Schnook University is doing a thesis on you, why should that give him a case of blueballs? The Letters are one department, a thesis is another. Tsk, tsk, these temperamental prima dons!

Waaal, I've got enough new poems, over the past three years, for a big fat book, not a slim one, including the Belli translations, if they don't get published in a volume of their own because everybody is getting cold feet about them. Only thing is, who'd publish my volume? I think I should have one out by next year, or nobody will know I exist. If I collect them sometime in the next six months, can I send them to you, and if you like them sufficiently, could you recommend them to David McDowell? I think you'll like the new stuff much more than the first book. I hope so.

Glad to hear that Horace Gregory's Horace appeals to you. Frankly, his Catullus, of the Twenties, couldn't be worse. He misses everything—the form, the tone, the spirit, the language, and instead of Catullus' frank, clear, hard edges there is only Gregory's version of *vers libre*, with soft decadent-Rome weary sensuality, something true of the American imitators of Imagism in the Twenties, but not, certainly, pre-Augustan Rome, at least not Catullus, whose bi-sexuality, as evidenced in those masterly verses, reflected a *norm* rather than a deviation, or a Puritan mockery, of sex. Unless one grasps the fundamentally amoral nature of sexual desire, in all its unconscious or pre-conscious force, one cannot understand, much less translate, a poet like Catullus, whose epoch was free of the abstract Christian

confusion that has already ruined forever our understanding
of what it is that makes Catullus so great. And Sappho,
whom he imitated and translated. How can we understand
(except individually, not as a society) an age in which one
of its leaders, speaking before a senatorial court, says: "If
anyone thinks that free intercourse, even with prostitutes, is
to be denied to youth, he is severe indeed; I cannot gainsay
him; this, however, I must say, that he differs not only from
the freedom of the present age, but likewise from what our
fathers practised and allowed. Was there ever a time when
it was not done? When it was condemned as a fault?
When it was not tolerated? In a word, was there ever a
time when a thing allowable was not allowed?" I hold that
speech to be as important as the Gettysburg Address! It
was not Lincoln; it was Cicero. And he was speaking about
Clodia, Catullus' girl friend, known in his poems as Lesbia.
Imagine President Eisenhower or, better, the Chief Justice
of the Supreme Court, whoever he is, making a speech like
that! If we can imagine it, then we can imagine a Twentieth
Century Catullus, and not otherwise. And Gregory misses
the boat for all these reasons. Poor Catullus is still not
translated into English; he will have to wait for a more
enlightened age than ours. I've done some straightforward
translations, but nobody will touch them. Anyway, Horace
is another bucket of fish, and I'll try to get hold of
Gregory's trans. which I haven't seen.

My best to you and Floss.

Ciao,
Hal

William C. Williams
9 Ridge Road
Rutherford, N.J.
Sept. 25, 1956

Dear Hal:

A really remarkable letter, I won't take the time to answer it now—if I ever can. Your characterization of the times of Catullus is worth much to me, I'll read that part over and over again. I have to confess to a piece of gross carelessness in speaking of Gregory's translation from the Latin as the works of "Horace" when I should have said Catullus. I'm ashamed of myself and hope you can overlook the error.

Send your book of poems on to me, I'll do my best to place them with Random House. The reason I cooled off on my delight over the Belli translations was that I lost some of my respect for Belli as a poet and a person after looking him up. The sonnet form as you know well doesn't intrigue, the translation will look better when there are more of them in a book.

Your illness worries me. I hope you will not have a cold winter in Italy next year. I want to get this letter off to you at once so I won't continue longer.

Best
Bill

Florence
30/9/56

Dear Bill,

Fancy that! It was Catullus, after all, and not
Horace...well, you're certainly forgiven for the blunder!
Only thing, if you knew how straightforward, direct, hard
and clear Catullus is in the original, you'd never have
forgiven Horace Gregory for window- dressing him the
way he does. The great Latin poet never pulled any verbal
punches, and even shocked the Roman society of his day,
which, I'm telling you, was hard to do! And his bi-sexuality
was not an act—he was even Julius Caesar's boyfriend for a
while, it seems, and that great man himself once declared
that he was "the husband of all the wives and the wife of all
the husbands in Rome." Well, how can we ever understand
them? What they took naturally we feel to be *contra naturam*,
against nature. And who is to say? It was the medieval
priests who invented all that stuff, including the cult of the
Holy Virgin—because the lawless barons of the middle
ages were treating women like whores, the priests had to do
something about it. "To render a Don Juan possible," says
Stendhal, "there must be hypocrisy in society."

"A Don Juan would have been an effect without a cause
in the ancient world; religion was a matter for rejoicing, it
urged men to take their pleasure; how could it have
punished people who make a certain pleasure their whole
business in life? The government alone spoke of *abstinence*,
it forbade things that might harm the state, that is to say
the common interest of all, and not what might harm the

individual actor."
The Cenci (Stendhal)

I'm writing a long series of poems on the Cenci, based on Stendhal's *nouvelle*. And before long, I'll send you an incomplete set of poems for the projected new book . I want to get them placed in magazines, as you suggest, before trying for a book. But it won't harm to interest Random House in the meanwhile.

I'm trying for a Guggenheim again, on the same project, the Belli translations. They make me sick, the grants and foundations. It will never change. All the gravy keeps going to the information-hunters and the second-rate poets.

Arrivederci,
Harold

American Express
Viajes Hispania
Esplanada, 3
Alicante, SPAIN
1/7/57

Dear Bill,

It has been a long time since I've heard from you. No answer to my last letter. Hope all's well, and here's a big HAPPY NEW YEAR to you and Floss, even though a week late.

I'm down here in the South of Spain where the sun

shines, thank God, really *hot* by day, and a bit cool by
night. But I have a terrific suntan in January; today, for
instance, I would say the thermometer read 90°F in the sun.
Amazing! My monthly bill for pension, i.e. room, service,
and food, is 45 bucks—240 pesetas! That's pretty good,
these days. I can manage, at that rate, to hang around here
until March 1st, then slowly wend my way to Malaga,
Granada, Seville, up to Madrid, Galicia, and then along the
South of France, Languedoc, Provence and finally back to
Italy by the middle or end of April. And I do it on a
shoestring. The shoestring is supplied by a wealthy patron.
I haven't got a shoestring of my own. And no strings
attached. He's a really cultured man, he thinks a lot of my
work, and thanks to him, I didn't die during my
convalescence which, it seems, is still continuing after that
nasty close call in Rome last winter.

Did you see my poem "Florence" in the Nov. POETRY?
And the prose excerpts from a book I'm writing on Italy
(December POETRY)? I really have quite a pile of new
stuff, and will be sending it around.

One of the few hopes I entertain for the new work is
that you'll like it. Or at any rate, some of it. I can't mail
you any because most of them are long and my biggest and
most dangerous expense is Air Mail postage to the USA.

Would love to hear from you and know how things are
going. I still haven't found a publisher for the Belli in book
form. But, then, I haven't tried. That is, Grove turned it
down last year, you told me that Random House wouldn't
touch it, etc.

I'm going to take a trip to Palma de Mallorca, which is
just off the coast here, in the Spring, and contact the Divers
Press. Do you know that outfit? I used to know Paul

Blackburn in New York. I think he's connected with it.

By the way, until you translated Quevedo, I had never heard of him. I never heard of him since, until the other day, at the pension, the old *proprietario* ripped off some really funny bawdy stories about him. It seems he was relieving himself by squatting on the floor of one of the royal palace rooms when a grand lady came in unexpectedly and exclaimed, "Quevedo! Quevedo!" He looked up and said, "She knows my name, but she doesn't even know the word for Shit!" (The pun on "Que vedo?"— what do I see?)

Affectionately,
Harold

William C. Williams M.D.
9 Ridge Road
Rutherford, N.J.
Jan. 24, 1957

Dear Hal:

At last! after all the excitement I have been in a mood to answer which could not be done hurriedly involving as it does a reading of your latest poems published in *Poetry*. Just last night I had to attend a meeting of the French Hospital Alumni Association and speak to the men. I graduated from my internship on the staff 50 years ago and have not attended a meeting since that date! Today I have to go to the city again for the official conferring of the award I have just received in poetry.

Glad you are in a warmer climate this year than last. God bless your sponsor who has made it possible. You poets and artists starving in Europe certainly do get around, bitter as it often is for you and tough as you have to be to survive.

The poems, which I read myself yesterday, had a curious effect on me. They disturbed me. It is not the sort of thing I could ever in this century understand. They are unique constructions seemingly from the quatro cento—or however you spell it.

Are they good or bad, a reader has to make up his mind. They are certainly not the usual thing. They have been most carefully studied for an especial effect, as much as to say, much in the past exceeds the present as babies exceed their elders.

Your vision and stress upon the savage masculinity or maleness of the times of the old masters is a masterly observation. That poem in which you speak of it here is frightening and will be totally ignored. They will not know what to do with it, it will be buried. It must not be because nowhere in my life or reading has an image been so vividly presented. I have never seen anything like it from the technique of its presentation to the understanding of what has been presented. It is really a masterpiece.

But as in any other masterpiece it incurs responsibilities. You can't repeat it. Are you going to change your style to conform to it? It may be. For you can't ignore what has been done. You as I see you are standing at a crossroads of your life. This poem is a beginning or an end, you can't remain inactive. The vision of the past you have presented has to be equaled in your own life—and the life of the world—or you and it will be lost. What you have done in this poem is too beautiful to ignore. In other words I conclude you must build on this magnificent poem developing and varying the lead to its full development or break from it completely. That poem has to stand alone. Go on from there. It's a risk but a risk that has to be taken.

McDowell is quitting Random House and founding with Ivan Obolensky a publishing house of his own. It may be a movement of tremendous importance to me and my friends. When I hear more I'll tell you.

Best
Bill

29 January, 1957

Dear Bill,

Your letter brought tears to my eyes. It is now six or seven years since you first singled out my work for your special praise, and since that time, it is always you, among American poets, who continues to see something unusual enough in my development to evoke, from time to time, your confidence and encouragement.

I am forty now, I have been writing since the age of six, I have a small magazine sort of reputation, I am not taken seriously, I have won no prizes and been given no fellowships, my only book of poems attracted no brass bands. I don't even think I deserved more than that, or at any rate, not more than most poets who are worth anything at all usually receive (at the start) at the hands of critics, professors and fellowship committees. But the gravy, most of it, does go to the smooth fellows who are fashionable and not too daring in their work. And I have never been fashionable, and I have always taken chances of one kind or another, in trying to be true to my experience of life as expressed in my poetry. No brass bands. No dough.

But aside from you, who notices me at all? Tate—he is a fine man, and has been encouraging, but not with your spontaneous kind of personal warmth and power to *believe* in someone else's struggle, and to assist him in it. Shapiro— nice guy, again, but aside from having published me, he doesn't help; Cummings—big person, big poet, but also big *noli me tangere*—one-life-to-a-customer-so-make-the-most-of-your-own. Which is perfectly true, too. I am not asking for anything from anyone. But it would be nice to know I exist for them. And this is what you make one feel, that's all. That one, as a poet, exists. And I don't mean mere publication, but exists in the only sense of the word—as a POET. And for this, I shall always be grateful that I know you.

You are right. I am at a crossroads. It was very keen of you to see it in the poem, "Florence", I mean the direction I had to take from there on. I think I am taking it by reliving the past, personal and cultural, and hope that I can make it live in my poetry, and then, God willing, go on from there. It is a way of turning away from all the dryrot in the present and establishing one's roots with the *live* elements of the past. It is a delicate way of going and of writing, and if kept alive, not museum-fashion, but as one's own past is alive in the present, it can be of special poetic value.

My sponsor, God bless him, read your last two books of poems, that you inscribed for me, and cried: "This man is great! He is a master! How is it that we in England haven't heard of him?!" The point is, there is almost nothing of real value in literature, in any language, and in the original, that is unknown to him. He is an Armenian with an Oxford background and with immense understanding in poetry. He read only a few lines of THE DESERT MUSIC when he made the above statements. I told him all about you, and he said he felt that if such a man as yourself had inscribed your books to me and believed in my work, then he felt he had really discovered something by discovering me. He made no bones about your work—far better than Pound or Eliot, whom he knows backwards. What you have done, according to him (and to me) is to keep the language alive by never for one second getting away from the colloquial. He cited Catullus, Rimbaud, Rilke, Homer, and others as the living colloquial tradition. He knows them in the original. Well, they are, after all, the best company. I hope I can join you in this company one day. It will have to come naturally. Until then, I do what I can.

The news about David McDowell and the new publishing company sounds magnificent. I hope, when it is formed, you will remember my Belli translations and my new poems for a book, or maybe two books. No one else is paying any attention to me or the translations, so maybe we can put one over on all of them!

I'll be here until the end of February, and then return to Florence some time in March. Keep me posted. I feel light years away from America and the literary world. That may be all to the good!

Muchas gracias for the good words and

Salud!
Harold

My best to Floss

William C. Williams M.D.
9 Ridge Road
Rutherford, N.J.
St. Valentine's Day
[14 February 1957]

Dear Hal:

Sometimes I think your place should be in NY, not
Europe. Then again I think just the opposite. What the
hell have I to do with it, you're the judge of what is best for
you. The cause of this outburst is a movement that began
in San Francisco among a group of young (not so young)
poets who are beginning to make their way at present in
New York. They are headed by Allen Ginsberg, Jack
Kerouac, a Canadian partially American Indian prose writer
who is soon to have a voluminous novel published by a
prominent house under the patronage of Malcolm Cowley;
you'll see more of that in the news later.

The reason I speak of that gang now is that the whole
gang of them is at present headed for Italy. Look for them
in a month around Florence and Rome, 4 or 5 of them
including a poet named Corso, the youngest of all who is
slowly making his presence felt around here, a very gentle
guy who has been through some very tough years out of
the slums of Brooklyn.

A feature of the united front that these men present is
that they are all Zen Buddhists, one of their most influential

members is at the present time living in a monastery in Japan. As you may run into the gang this spring in Italy I wanted you to know in advance about them. They are self-sufficient and ask nothing for themselves—they usually carry knapsacks out of which they live. I hope you meet at least one of them for they know what they are about and you would enjoy meeting them.

But.

Right at this time when you yourself have just struck a lead may not be profitable to dwell too much on Allen Ginsberg and his gang, I thought I'd mention him at least.

Your last letter really moved me. I'll speak to Dave McDowell as soon as I think he has had a chance to get settled in his new job. Meanwhile I look to see more poems, a bookful, exploiting what you have begun of the interrelationship of the renaissance & the modern.

More power to you
Bill

If you *will* not put your address on the letters you send to me how can I help it if the mere envelopes are destroyed?
Bill

Luckily Floss kept the envelope for the stamps.
Bill

NO ADDRESS
(am leaving this
place to travel around Spain)
23rd February, 1957

Dear Bill,

Many thanks for your last. It is odd that you should have said, referring to where I should be, the same as my Armenian friend, who writes as follows: "From what I have been able to observe these last years, it seems that your mode of writing follows its own laws of development and is therefore best let to follow its own bent. Ultimately, you are feeling your way towards a style of utmost and crystal clarity, of which the Florentine poems already give a foretaste. But for the definitive form of this the time is not yet; therefore in the following representative poems [a very long new poem which I will send you in a month or so from Florence], i.e. those you sent me, you move to a greater density and complexity in language, in rime and alliteration, in syntax. This shows that your subconscious knows what it is doing, and there is no call for any of us to intervene. You will probably go through various stages of alternate simplicity and complexity before you reach your own definitive clarity as Williams seems to have done, for instance, in his latest work."

I believe I mentioned this Armenian sage in an earlier letter, saying that when he read *The Desert Music* and *Journey to Love*, which you inscribed to me, he was astonished and said, "Why don't we in England hear more of this man? He is really great—far better than Pound or Eliot!" At any rate, he is my sponsor—God bless him!—and also a kind of mentor. I bring him up because it all ties together: Europe, my poetry, Buddhism. It is strange, very strange that in your last letter you should mention Allen Ginsberg and his Buddhist bunch. I hadn't heard of his Buddhism, but knew Ginsberg slightly some twelve years ago. We met in the

subway at about four a.m. We were the only occupants of
the car, and he was leaning back drunkenly reciting
Rimbaud, I think, in French, and we got to talking and
bumped into each other once or twice since then. At any
rate, one of the main reasons for my being in this isolated
town on the coast of Spain was to concentrate heavily on
Buddhist works, which I have done. IS IT STRANGE? I
am not a Zen Buddhist, but I am receptive and sympathetic.

My place, dear Bill, is right here for the time being—
Europe. It has brought out the best in me, that might never
have come into being had I not left the States, which, I can
say, had brought out the worst in me. When the time is
ripe, I shall return. Meantime, whatever developments
occur in my poetry, I owe to Europe, to the Armenian
sponsor-mentor, to an inner growth and artistic inner
revival that would have surely been crushed out of me,
crushed to death, in New York. That is why I fled New
York. The city, the people; they were certain death, I knew
it. It was all or none. Stay and die, or leave and take my
chances. The second proved to be my sheer physical, as
well as mental, survival.

Yes, I have struck a lead, and it has been going, thank
God, smoothly, according to its own laws. I myself am
only dimly beginning to perceive where the poetry is
going—I just let it go, and then I see where it has taken me!
I have now a book, a big book—some 60 poems, with a
basic theme: the interrelationship of the past with the
modern, as seen through experiences with time and place.
A good half of the book, like the Florence poems, treats of
place, where personages and events move through
landscapes and cities in a constant voyage. There are many
long poems. But the whole thing I will have to whip into

shape in Florence, where I shall be returning in April. I'm glad you will speak to David McDowell about this, when the time is ripe.

Meanwhile, if you see any of the Buddhist boys, before their departure for these shores, don't hesitate to tell them to look me up in Florence. I'd like to see Allen Ginsberg again, and I've heard of Corso. I, too, come from the slums of Brooklyn. One never knows what a slum will produce.

I have no address now, and will be dropping you a line on picture postcards from various Spanish towns, to gladden your heart!

So keep up the good work, may we all enter the pearly gates in due time!

All the best,
Hal
&, of course, to Floss!

Via Santo Spirito 32
c/o Kimball
Florence, Italy
April 30, 1957

Dear Bill,

I'm glad to see you have some poems in HUDSON REVIEW, where you thought, because they had once written something knocking you, that they were agin you. Well, they ain't. And may all the world love you, and God bless you forever!

Morgan, of HUDSON, is also Field Editor for

Princeton University Press, and has asked for the complete Belli translations, recommending [that they] publish them in book form, along with your Introduction, and the one on Belli by Moravia, which he gave me. So let us pray, Bill, that the other editors will find them publishable, along with the "dirty" ones—which you haven't seen, and sound like Henry Miller at his funniest dirtiest. They ought to have a tremendous sale, if published, so long as the bluenoses don't get after the book and make trouble. Pray, pray, pray—for I need a break of some kind. *And* money.

How come you haven't answered my last two letters that I sent from Spain??? The last one I got from you, you said you would talk to McDowell about publishing my next book of poems, which is almost ready, now. I've got some long poems to finish up. *Les jeunes*, namely, Louis Simpson and Robert Pack, have discovered me (*les jeunes* my ass, Simpson is four or five years younger than I, and that either makes him middle-aged or me middle-young or something).

Just for the record: I sent him some poems when he was guest editor of poetry for *New World Writing* and the poems arrived too late to be considered. Here are some of the things he wrote me: "I have seen your work in some of the magazines...and admire it. There is no doubt that you are one of the small number of outstanding poets, with an exceptional and original gift. It is strange that you should be submitting your poems to me; it is quite likely that in a year or so I will be submitting mine to you...If the poems had been here earlier, I would gladly have included either 'Freak' or 'Lines for a Beggar'. But there is nothing I can do about it now." And so on. This is an unusual reply from an editor, and was heartening to receive at the time, but I have again sunk into a private hole in the ground of my own making, no doubt, for every time I pick up an American little mag, somebody or other is getting a grant, an award, MONEY—from the little mags themselves, where I, too, publish, or from the foundations straight off. And this is what pisses me off. You'd think I didn't exist.

Anyway, let's hear from you soon. Would McDowell be interested in the Belli book, just in case the editors at Princeton U Press get cold feet—remember, it's DIRTY!!

Warmest to you & Floss,
Harold

P.S. I'm enclosing the last poem (the one Simpson saw) from a group called "Lines for a Beggar".

P.S.S. I am waiting for a final reply on the Belli book from Frederick Morgan, who wrote as follows:

"Your Belli ms. arrived safely...the day before I was to make a trip to Princeton. I took the ms. with me, and have left it with them with the recommendation that we publish it. However, I would prefer that the final selection have around one hundred rather than only fifty poems, and if the others agree with me on this we may be asking you to translate more. I would not advise you to go ahead now though until we are sure that the Press is definitely interested. I look forward to receiving the prefaces by Williams and Moravia as soon as possible."

If I had to sit down and translate fifty more, it would take me about six months—let's say a year—and to do this I would have to have a grant. HUDSON REVIEW, of which Morgan is chief editor, has been given a Rockefeller subsidy and is offering grants, yet Morgan has made no mention to me of this. One way of getting them is to have an established poet recommend you for the grant. Since you have written the Preface to my Belli, could you write a nice sort of letter to Morgan about putting me up for the next HUDSON Fellowship in poetry—basing this on my past performance, but especially for the job of going on with the Belli translations? These guys have to be handled tactfully, Bill—they're rich. And that's saying enough. So let me know if you do this. As usual, you are the only literary figure who's ever tried to do anything for me. God bless you,

Hal

William C. Williams
9 Ridge Road
Rutherford, N.J.
May 6, 1957

Dear Hal:

The last letter, possibly the last two letters, I sent you, to Spain, must never have reached you. I can't hold myself responsible for that. I'll write at once to Morgan and when I hear from him again I'll let you hear what he says. The Beli (or is it Belli?) translations interested me very much and should be published. I hope Princeton will do it. But the last poems from *Poetry* were, in my opinion, the best I have seen of yours in years. I can't understand why you have not been able to get some grant.

Dave McDowell is for the time being at least not

interested in poetry. I spoke to him about the Belli translations but he was not interested. His is too young a house with too many commitments of his own for me to want to push him where he may not want to go. I have not forgot you, when I am talking with him I'll remind him of your name.

No, the Morgan lead strikes me as likely to be best. I'll push it as hard as I can. Let's see what happens. You know of course that *Hudson Review* is to publish my long short story "The Farmers' Daughters" in August. I have waited long for that. I am not writing much otherwise but for reviews. I feel sometimes as if I'm all washed up, haven't felt the inclination to do a poem in months, the poetic yen is gone—or maybe my philosophy has turned too much toward the acceptance of what life dishes out to me in these final few years.

I am too sympathetic with women and do not want them anymore except in the head. Men disgust me with their "science". There is a programme on the air featuring a child of 10 who can answer any question in higher mathematics, physics or astronomy that can be put to him. Really remarkable. I'm waiting to have him tried on love to have a report on his little penis, [if it] will take over to piece [out] the work of his brain. I'm getting too old to care. I know damned well that my own prick no longer reacts to anything, useless except to piss out of and not even reliable for that.

Yours
Bill

Via Santo Spirito 32
c/o Kimball
Florence, Italy
August 26, 1957

Dear Bill,

I haven't heard from you in so long I'm beginning to
think that even you, of all people, have forgotten me. The
last letter I had from you must have been at least eight
months ago. In it, you said something about McDowell
being too filled up on commitments now to be approached
on the subject of a book of poems. But to have patience.
To wait. *Pazienza*, says Norman Douglas somewhere, can
be translated as: *It's hopeless!*

I am waiting. I am also writing. I have at least three
books of poems on my hands, counting the Belli
translations as one. Naturally, the Princeton University
Press welshed on the deal. They got cold feet. Always the
same story. They're afraid of the dirty words, afraid of the
old-fashioned home-truths about popes, governments,
sexual abuses, etc. When will the fuckin Anglo-Saxons
grow up??! All those dirty poems of Belli against the Pope
are in the Vatican Library, where they are enjoyed by the
clergy and people alike. In fact, they were published under
the Papal Government. Latins are so much more adult than
Anglo-Saxons that it will take at least another millennium
for them to grow up, if at all. Meanwhile, nobody is
handing me any fellowships to get on with the Belli
translations.

I certainly seem to be beefing. But in spite of all the
money in America, I continue to write—and in spite of all

the little magazines, which are now fully brought round, by the universities, to conformity and convention—since the universities support most of them and the rich support the universities—I continue to write as I please. Oh, I have quite a reputation, it seems, among other poets, older and younger, who are in the swim and known more widely. But from this distance, it grows harder and harder, it seems, for me to cut any ice on the American scene. Hope all's well with you. For God's sake, let me know how things are! Best to you and Floss,

As ever,
Harold

Via Santo Spirito 32
c/o Kimball
Florence, Italy
24/10/57

Dear Bill,

This is a brief one to find out how you are and whether all is well. I certainly hope so, not having heard from you in a blue moon. I remember writing you several times. I hope you've been too busy to answer, but that you may find a minute or two soon.

I noticed that the Thirlwall book of your letters finally came out, and that reviews have been marvellous. Congratulations! I, of course, am too far away to lay my hands on a copy, and not in a position to order one. Are the letters to me included?? Thirlwall had said he would use several as examples of different types, or something to that effect. I would love to have a copy of the book.

I continue writing, teaching, but feel left out and far away. I am trying to arrange getting back to New York early next year, and if I can swing it, one of the first things I want to do is rush out to Rutherford and take up as much of your time as you will let me, talking to you. You have no idea how much that would mean. I'm so tired of all the idiots that get sent over here on Fulbrights and Guggenheims and pass for scholars, painters, etc., the whole lot of 'em not worth ten cents, believe me. They are the most stiff-necked, snot-nosed, flat-footed crew in all Europe. You can pick out a Fulbright in the streets of Florence and Rome as easily as you can spot a Harvard man in Scully Square. "Full pockets and heads empty as shells", as I wrote in some poem after Catullus.

I expect to send out a lot of poems before long, as they have been piling up, and after or if they get published, submit a book or two to some publisher in the States. I suppose David McDowell, as you once suggested, is still all booked up??? Let me know.

All the best to you and Floss,

As ever,
Harold

William C. Williams
9 Ridge Road
Rutherford, N..J.
Oct. 31/57

Dear Harold:

Let's not quarrel about the times I write you and you do not receive the letters. At present I have had my back to the wall relative to correspondence. The letters have been partly to do with that, their success has (for me) been phenomenal. Everybody and his uncle has written me letters, mostly strangers of no distinction but requiring answers.

Then *Paterson 5* had to be finished, etc., and then came a bid or a summons from the U. of California to subject myself as a robot to their Institute of Personality [Assessment and Behavior] something or other to be "studied"...we're going there now to remain 3 weeks, etc. etc. I'm waiting momently to receive the copies of *Hudson Review* containing my long delayed long short story, "The Farmers' Daughters." I'll send you reprints just as soon as I receive them. And, a copy of the letters just as soon as I can get Dave McDowell to mail it to you.

Glad you're planning to cross to the States soon. Good bye young man, it's not all lost while you still have the will to go on.

Bill

Glad you're teaching, first you've told me of that.

Via Santo Spirito 32
c/o Kimball
Florence, Italy
2 December, 1957

Dear Bill,

It was a great relief to hear from you! I realize that you must have had, and still are having, a terrible responsibility, not to say drain on your time and energy, answering all those letters from people who've read your published ones. At least, it's a sign that poets, although they can't hold their own against the popularity of film stars, are not entirely without an appreciative audience—like any audience, composed of a few really sensitive and intelligent ones, the rest autograph-hunters. Well, it's something!

Thanks for thinking about sending me a reprint of HUDSON with "The Farmers' Daughters" and also a copy of the letters. I look forward to them. I'm curious also to know the results of your "Personality Test"—or should I say "rating"?—at the U. of Cal. Just *what* part of the body do they measure???

I didn't know there was going to be a *Paterson 5*, but that's exciting news. DO you intend to have other sections to follow? Have you got a plan for the whole? Really, Bill, one of the few chief reasons why I want to come back—if I can swing it financially—is to see you again. I am now beginning to realize, much as I love it here, that I am getting out of touch with that which, in the end, matters most to me—namely, the most important people in one's life. Of course, I have that here—but they are not of the same background. And one's language belongs to that.

Morgan, of HUDSON, wrote some time ago saying he was coming to Europe and would look me up here to discuss the chances of working up interest in the Belli translations as a volume. Have never seen hide nor hair.

Have two original volumes of poetry on my hands, looking for a publisher: FIGURES FOR AN ITALIAN DANCE and MUSIC FOR THE RIGHT WORDS. I have

one pupil whom I teach for two bucks an hour, three times
a week. I supplement it with a part-time patron. Yes, I've
still got the will to go on—in times like these, what else can
one have? I've never run into the Ginsberg gang, by the
way.

All the best to you and Floss,

Harold
Season's Greetings!

Via Santo Spirito 32
c/o Kimball
Florence, Italy
24/12/57

Dear Bill,

The top of the year to you, and may you have many of
them!

Things are humming along here—and sometimes
hawing—but all in all, let's say they're looking up a bit. A
poem of mine has just been taken for the next issue of
NEW WORLD WRITING. Another, of about 125 lines,
was taken by COMMENTARY and set up in proofs before
I had time to look around. In the meantime, Jonathan
Williams of Jargon Books is writing to me about the Belli
manuscript, and seems to think he will take a chance on it,
although I warned him he might have the police on his tail.
Let's hope the new year will bring me a little more
recognition.

Awaiting your book of Letters and also your story "The

Farmers' Daughters" in HUDSON REVIEW.

Jean Garrigue is coming from Rome and will stay with me here in Florence, and we should have a very creative winter, as I see too little of my poet-friends, the few I have, and need just such a thing right now anyway to put me back in touch, so to speak. Although there are times, many of them, when I feel that the solitary worker in the AHHHTS is the one in closest touch with what counts. There is too much confusion in everything today for the poets to run around in groups, or herds, and they usually imagine that by protection of this kind they will insulate themselves from the dirty world, but what usually happens is they set up a body politic of their own, and begin to sound like one another. BAAAA...

Is David McDowell ever going to get interested in new volumes of poetry? I have at least three, all ready for the press. Four and a half years of hard labor, yes sir. And I'm just sticking my head out of the rockpile now, with a few choice nuggets.

Again, all the best for the holidays, to you and Floss, and drop me a line when you can extricate yourself from that mound of letters you have to send to all those who are now craving an autograph.

Best,
Hal

William C. Williams
9 Ridge Road
Rutherford, N.J.
Jan. 7/58

Dear Hal:

G. or Jean Garrigue is a fine name for me to here link with your sojourn this winter in Italy, I believe in that girl and am impressed by the poems she is writing of late. You should have good times there together.

The news seems generally good or better than it has been in recent years. Glad you received the things I forwarded to you. The news that Jonathan Williams is, on the other hand, giving up *Jargon*, not so good. Keep out of this country as long as you can eat! It's poison to the intellectual. It's going to get worse for many years to come, in my opinion, or just as long as money governs the conduct of our lives. Can *you* see any end to that juggernautery? The horrible sight of our swollen cars that infest our roads should be enough for any man who has kept a vestige of his brains about him .

The translation of Belli's sonnets should be read by everyone in America, that nascent home of the new Catholicism, but it won't be published if the priests can prevent it, and they are becoming more and more powerful here.

Nothing I can do about getting your poems published by McDowell, Obolensky, especially because Dave has often told me that for the first year at least the firm cannot afford to indulge themselves in any poetry—unless *Paterson* 5 should be offered them but that is now unlikely.

Stick to Garrigue, may she guide you through the months to come. Keep well.

Sincerely yours
Bill

Via Santo Spirito, 32
c/o Kimball
Florence, Italy
1/22/58

Dear Bill,

Many thanks for your kindness in sending reprints of "The Farmers' Daughters" and the essay in the *American Scholar* and the *Selected Letters*. The short story set me back on my heels. After gabbling in Italian, French, Spanish and German for four and a half years, the breath of raw American speech made me remember it (of course, half of the time I'm talking to Americans, there seems to be more of them here than in the whole USA, and each of them with a Fulbright—and the language they speak is a mixture of Ph.D. and American Express—"Didja look *cair*-fly?? been expectin a letter from my Ant Hepsy for weeeeks"). As I say, those rural daughters of yours, cut so dissectingly on the run, reminded me that American language still lives, even if it left me with a desire not to encounter that type in the flesh, since it fills me with a kind of horror of the void, the great thrashing American vacuum, which is filled with a squamous kind of desperation, since Nature herself abhors a vacuum, and there's little to fill it with, if you're a farmer's daughter, except a man.

I liked the essay very much. That kind of honesty, which is your water-mark, freshens up the reader who is exposed too much to either knotty, crabbed literary thinking or academic tedium.

The *Letters*, which I have glanced through, left me deeply disappointed and boiling mad. Not, of course, at you—and nothing to do with the letters themselves—but with the unspeakable Thirlwall, who if he keeps it up will be nudging Oscar Williams out of the rathole.

Why, in Heaven's name, WHY did he make me spend good liras in stamp money and go riffling through my cardboard boxes in New York hunting out your letters to me, if he didn't use a single one?? There are at least 50 of them, those you have sent me here in the four and a half years I've been in Europe, and those in New York. And among them, literary documents, a side of your character which, I think, was not in evidence in the book as selected—the direct, humane, compassionate, human side. Yes, yes, that's in the book too, it remains in anything you write, and maybe I'm speaking from irritation and the sense of being left out of everything.

If I am left out of a connection with W.C. Williams, the only major poet who has ever budged to help me in any way, then where do I come in??? It feels like treachery, and I don't mind telling that louse Thirlwall so. I noticed he gave a full representation to himself (Shades of Oscar W.). And he had told me he was using four or five!

Anyway, there's compensation in the fact that my work is getting published. The current January issue of ART NEWS is carrying a poem of mine, "Monet's Venice"; NEW WORLD WRITING 13, forthcoming issue, is carrying another, "Almonds Like Pink Snow", and COMMENTARY will publish a long poem called "Roman Ghetto" and two anthologies will show my Belli translations and other original work. Meanwhile, I have a whole new book of poems that I'm sending off to Scribner's today, Wheelock has shown an interest, and although I'm not wild about having 85 typewritten pages of poetry appear in a book with two other poets (POETS OF TODAY), still where else can I send it? You tell me Dave McDowell is booked up on poetry, so what alternative is there? If Wheelock takes it, I'll be grateful. At least, it will be seen and I'll have crawled from the underbrush where I've been hiding. In your letters somewhere you say that Eliot and Pound had given you the feeling that you were down in the jungle jumping about with the monkeys, while they were in some upper stratosphere, etc. Well, you can imagine what I must feel like—as if the monkeys themselves were in the stratosphere, and I looking up. Literary politics is the foulest game of all, and I've never played it any more than you have. But if I've got anything at all, I would like to see it get some attention .

The chief problem, as I see it, is how to strike out for a new metric, a new line, cadence, rhythm, whatever you may call it, and avoid the strictures of the so-called iambic. My work in the book of poems up till now (four and a half years) shows my own enslavement to iambics, but also my struggle against this, and if the musical phrase is another step away, where does one go from there? Whitman, you say, is too loose, without metrics, but if he indicates the need to break with the ti-tum-ti-tum-ti-tum-ti-tum, where can one go without losing the poetry somewhere along the way? Between prose rhythm and poetry rhythm there is a fine line. Have you or Pound or Marianne Moore or Eliot—all of you in one way or another showing a new cadence—have you gone as far as it is possible to go without losing the rhythm poetry must have?? And is that why the poets of the 40's and 50's have gone back to metronomes??? You seem to admire Lowell, but he's in the strict tradition of "iambic pentameter", the old English five-beat rising rhythm, for all his wonderful sense of phrasing, condensation, contained violence of measure and imagery—like Crane in this, using the traditional measure but making it personal.

And is Allen Ginsberg doing anything really NEW—or is it the long Biblical measureless Whitman line, again, with a violence of diction and content?

Jean Garrigue is here in Florence and we see each other at least twice a day, for lunch and dinner, and go to concerts, art galleries, etc. She sends you her best as do I, to both you and Floss.

As ever,
Hal

P.S. Would there be any use in my sending you my book of poems— if you could interest McDowell, supposing Wheelock doesn't take it? Also for your own interest in same???

American Express
Florence, Italy
4/2/58

Dear Bill,

(Please note new mailing address above for future mail.)

Thanks for the letter & the good words about Jean Garrigue, who was delighted to hear them & she should be writing you any day now. She's reading the *Letters of WCW* which I lent her & finds it, as I do, very exciting (curses, however, on the sneaky Thirlwall for excluding your letters to me!)

I accept wholeheartedly what you say about "swollen [American] cars that infest our roads". I am trying to convince Jean to stay here in Italy (we've both been offered teaching jobs in Naples) but although morally she's for it, she hankers after the people she knows in the States, & is less of an explorer, perhaps, than I. Maybe you can convince her to stay at least a year. We stimulate each other, & are both getting into a new writing vein, reading our poems every night, criticizing, talking shop. It's great for me—I've missed that.

It looks like I can come to New York for a month this spring—I can't wait to see you! In fact, you're one of the chief reasons! But I'll be damn sure to have a return ticket! One month or so is all I'd be able to stand!

Where did you learn that Jonathan Williams is giving up Jargon?? He just asked me a couple of months ago for my Belli book & I just spent over 4 bucks to mail it to him! I hope you're wrong!!

I'm having poems accepted & will appear in *New World Writing, Paris Review, Commentary, Art News* (current January number), etc. I've sent my volume off to Scribner's for the "Poets of Today" series—where else can one send??

Keep well, & all my best & warmest to you & Floss!

Hal

William C. Williams M.D.
9 Ridge Road
Rutherford, N.J.
Feb. 11, 1958

Dear Hal:

Good news that you are coming to the States, we'll see you then for more than one jam session to keep up with the news, both ways. I'm glad that the traffic in poems has begun to pick up, at last, in your favor though I knew the writing of them has never ceased. The news about Jean Garrigue, your meeting and talking with her, makes me very happy. It's a rare chance that has brought you together in Italy, I'm glad you're making the most of it, we'll surely hear from that later in the work itself. Lucky kids.

Floss was hit by one of those cars (a small truck in this case) but fortunately not seriously, though painfully, injured. She's all right now. That didn't make me love the genus any better. But the swollen egos they represent, I'm afraid, only too accurately represent Americans of the present race. I don't like 'em, they are the ones who reject our poems in the main and piss on them if given the chance. Never give them a break if you come to have anything to do with 'em.

But it's swell that the Belli letters will finally be brought out, as you say, in all probability. The chance that you will be teaching in Naples next year is also encouraging. Go to it so you will be at least able to eat.

For myself I'm proposing a year of rest if I can bring myself to it. Now that *Pat.* 5 has been written I feel that I need it. Take care of yourself.

Bill

American Express
Florence, Italy
14/2/58

Dear Bill,

Thanks for the letter and amen to what you say about
the swollen egos and swollen cars. I am very sorry to hear
about Floss being run into by one of the monsters, but glad
she is better now. It does look as if it's getting worse all the
time, and no relief in sight. Now it is unemployment, the
usual turn of the wheel, the wheel of the vicious circle
called society. There is no hope, I'm afraid, that the greed
of men will abate in our time, so that all the savagery of
animal impulses will certainly be let loose again, and the
holocaust of terror increases. Ah, let us leave that bitter
note, for one cannot, if one thinks and feels, live with the
sword dangling over the head, and must go on as if it will
never drop.

I am sailing for New York on the 17th of March from
Naples, and expect to arrive on the 24th. I shall rest a
couple of days and then get in touch with you. Have you
got a phone, by the way? If you send me your number, I
can call you up. If not, I'll drop you a note from New York
and then we can get together for that wonderful jam
session. Jean Garrigue has been stimulated by our contact
to start writing again, poetry and a novel, and I have been

equally stimulated by her presence, all in all, a good
friendship. She sends you her best. I hope you will take
that year off and have a good rest, you deserve it. You have
already done enough that would do credit to three or two
ordinary lifetimes, so why not?

What you say about the idiots who run most of the
magazines is damn true, they are mostly unimaginative
gentlemen who have more to do with soap and toothpaste
than with literature and ought to stick to the former
without intruding their fat sleek bodies into the latter. I'm
sick of hypocritical, narrow-minded, bitter gentlemen. I'm
writing an attack, a satire, on Yvor Winters, one of the
worst, and hope to be able to publish it. It may help to hurl
ridicule at the ridiculous.

All my best to you and Floss, and hope to see you soon.

Affectionately,
Harold

573 Third Avenue
New York 16, New York
27/3/58

Dear Bill,

I'm back in Zombieland! Two days of it, and I feel like
an immigrant, frightened, over-awed, disgusted. The cars,
the swollen cars. And the skyscrapers, which I had seen for
five years only in my nightmares. A nightmare can come
true. Here I am, the dog in his vomit, between, from my
windows, the Empire State and the UN Building. And my

poor mother, who has aged so much I can hardly recognize her, a wrinkled cheerful monkey, chattering with pleasure and hopping about, has a "television" and a Crosley refrigerator, and thinks it's happiness. I sat and watched TV with her last night, and was choked up with bitterness and loathing at the commercials, the smooth dead tone of the announcers selling smooth dead machine-made horrors to an unthinking infantile population. She has turned my apartment into a three-room poor farm, and goes about in rags, doing her daily hard grind at the factory, saving a few miserable pennies for me, all for me, and my sense of guilt and shame is so suffocating I can hardly breathe. I smile and reassure her. All those palaces of the titled and wealthy friends I have in Rome, Florence and Naples, seem now like some huge deception OF MY SENSES, a five-year dream from which I have abruptly awakened, to find myself once again in the clean, innocent and ineluctable poverty into which I was born and from which I seem never to be able to rise. Curse it, spit on it, it is always there, it is what I come from, it is a cancer, a disease. But there is always Europe, where it is dignified and beautiful, where the poor have the sun and the clean unsmoky air, at least in Italy, and where the senses and the spirit can always breathe. In a few months, my mother will be eligible for old age insurance, I am trying to get her to go to California and live on it there, and then I hope the whole goddam incubus will dissolve finally and let me be.

Forgive this outburst, it is my first impression on my return. Now I know that I can never live here again, that I cannot wait to return, in six weeks, to Italy. I want to see you as much as I can while I'm here. We have a lot to say. Let me know when I can come out, and if you have a phone number, let me have it. At least, I shall see some publishers, some things of mine have been coming out in the mags, and I've got at least enough poems for three more volumes. NEW WORLD WRITING is bringing out a poem in the next number, June. I had a long poem in the February COMMENTARY.

Dear Bill, how glad I will be to see you! Best to Floss.

Warmly,
Harold

William C. Williams M.D.
9 Ridge Road
Rutherford, N.J.
April 4, 1958

Dear Hal:

Welcome home. We've been away over a week visiting friends up state and will be busy over the weekend with the family but after that come out as soon as you are able. Just call up and come—we'll accommodate ourselves as we [can]. No fuss. I am trying to do some translations of an anthology of Spanish poems for a Rutgers professor which will occupy my mornings for a while but we can take them in our stride.

My phone number is WE 3-1496. The best time to get me is around 1 o'clock.

It'll take me a couple of days to come to earth after my train trip which leaves my head whirling after it is over. Completely nuts. But I wanted to get this to you at once.

God knows what is waiting for me in as yet unopened letters.

My love to your staunch mother, it is cheering news that she will soon get her pension. More power to her. You are fortunate to be able to escape to Italy in six weeks. See you later.

Yours
Bill

William C. Williams M.D.
9 Ridge Road
Rutherford, N.J.
June 5, 1958

Dear Hal:

When I took up your poems and started to read this morning it was something of a shock. They or the one I read is farther off today's track than I had foreseen. It, the poem I speak of, is beautifully written but it is straight from Ovid or Lucretius. Nothing indicates that it comes from the present age—the meter, and that is the test that I apply, is completely undisturbed by the present.

You may say that that is exactly what you want, a recent poem by Cocteau presents the same problem to me: textually you are brothers, you follow classic modes: we Americans (as if you were not one of us) show a restlessness with the composition of the line itself and what its composition implies.

Call up sometime early next week, Floss says the pie

will be even better next time.

Sincerely,
Bill

I'll send your poems along with the batch sent me by you earlier back to you in a couple of days. Don't get me wrong, as of course you will not, thinking I have "rejected" them. Who the hell am I to reject work of yours? Come back at me having read *Pat. 5* and give me the hell I undoubtedly deserve but don't forget to return the script I lent you as it is not my own and Floss wants to keep it.

Bill

573 Third Ave
New York, N.Y.
Monday, 23/6/58

Dear Bill,

Have sent my MS under separate cover. Hope you have time to skim through—it's a large book. I'm leaving in two weeks, flying to London on July 7th. So I'll telephone next week. Hope all's well with you & Floss. As for me, I'm perverse—no sooner do I approach my wished-for departure than I decide I'd like to spend a year or two here! It's cuckoo!

Harold

William C. Williams M.D.
9 Ridge Road
Rutherford, N.J.
June 25, 1958

Dear Hal:

The poems hit me on an unlucky day. I didn't like
them. Everything about them irritated me. As always
under such circumstances I blame myself first. It began
with the dedication, please don't dedicate the book to
me—I'm only interested in one kind of verse and this is not
that kind.

Don't be sore at me. Perhaps I'm all wrong in my
preferences and have been wrong all my life in them. It is
all linked with my melioristic philosophy, I have all my life
believed in the perfectibility of man and so have been led
to believe in a constant conviction that if we are "good" and
free our intelligence will force us upon the subtlest devices
of art. Nothing can stop my experimentation with the
means at my disposal to make the words, my own medium,
move more freely in the sentence—and yet they must be
measured and disciplined. That is the problem.

The first poem in this collection was bad,
unquestionably awkwardly forced, the words made to
conform to some standard unrecognized by me. Such rigid
conformity to rule got my blood boiling at the start. You
didn't write that way when I first met you. Just the
opposite, you were wild but not ungoverned.

On the other hand, "The Prince", which was the first
one in this collection that convinced me of your undoubted
literary excellence, won me entirely. At the place toward

the end of the script marked, IV, beginning, "Meditation Over Snow", you show that you are putting most of your rigidities in their proper places.

It is difficult to speak of a poet's work critically, especially if he is a friend with whom you have been at all intimate. Nothing is to be gained by scanting the issues involved. Take care of yourself and if you still value my opinion and want to show me what you have been doing in Italy, come again. It might have been wise for your poetry's sake to spend another year or two in this country but who knows what the world is coming to, you may at that be better off in Italy. Take care of yourself. Floss joins me in sending you her love. The women have all the best of it in this man's world.

Affectionately yours
Bill

573 Third Avenue
New York 16, NY
27/6/58

Dear Bill,

Well, this is the reaction I really expected from you, and I'm glad you came out with it and got it off your chest and off mine, at the same time. When you had praised "Meditation Over Snow" and the "Procopius" so highly for being beautifully written, with command of language and richness, etc., I was embarrassed by your praise and truly baffled. I knew it was not your "kind of poetry". Now I know that you're not interested but "in one kind of verse and this is not that kind," as you say. Of course, I'll remove the dedication to you, as you request. I don't see as it should make any difference in our friendship. I've always put the work before anything else and shall continue to do so.

I'm not apologizing for the volume, I had to do it. The necessity behind writing in just this way was my necessity, and I feel that these poems have nothing in common with the academic kind of verse that is filling magazines today. Let me put it this way. I was "wild but not ungoverned" in my earlier work which you hailed. Then I felt the inner need to master the more rigid forms before taking a leap into the unknown, as I never felt *secure enough*, in every sense, to write loosely or colloquially or to undertake experiments with the line, meter, and *look* of the poem. And I think that most of the people who are doing that in my generation are simply repeating what Pound and Cummings and Moore and you did better several decades before them. And please remember: there are truly remarkable and first rate American poets who write strictly in the old hypnotic iambic pentameter—Crane, Robert Lowell, Frost, Stevens, Theodore Roethke, Shapiro, Schwartz, Ransom, and others. Of these I'm sure you admire Crane, Stevens, Lowell, Roethke—or am I wrong? In your published letters, at least, you speak very highly of Lowell in correspondence with him. What the hell has he added to meter? And Crane—complex, symbolistic, mystical—is great, the greatest American lyric poet of the century, for my money. I grew up literarily in the forties, and perhaps I would have done better to study poetry more carefully, but like Crane I simply took the line of least resistance and said what I had to say in iambics—which I, too, hate, and have been struggling to get farther away from—without success! It is a kind of link to the whole poetic tradition in English—a necessary evil, almost. But I think you misread my work. I think you misread the first poem in the book, & then the others, taking the cue from there. They come from a central emotion, a strong experience. The poems go from constriction—as in the first, which was dictated by necessity, the constriction of feeling—and then open out, as they go along, to a kind of freer rhythm and point to possibilities of individual experiment, not just taking over somebody else's voice and discoveries. I hope I am right, for if I'm not, I haven't gone anywhere. This book had to be done in this way because I could trust no other experience but my own. I was trying to learn how to write poetry by doing it, not by copying it. Look at Pound's influence and name ONE so-called poet influenced by him who is worthy of the name! Charles Olson? A pompous imitator who adds nothing. Who, in God's name, is there? Name one! And Creeley who imitates both of you, and that girl Denise Levertov—well, I guess you think she's good, but I can't see what she's done that changes the picture one little bit. I think May Swenson is a better poet than any of the people influenced by you or Pound, and she sometimes, but not often, sounds like Cummings. But isn't it strange that Roethke, in his long wild poems, sounds like nobody but Roethke, and uses fixed thumping iambics like Yeats with huge personal aplomb that makes them original; and that Lowell, who sounds like nobody else and has force and intellect and spirit and enormous command of language–has added nothing technically, certainly no more than Crane did. My

God, I'm willing to learn from anybody who can teach me!
Yes, the musical phrase that Pound uses or the "variable
foot" that you are formulating—these are also rules, and
they are your own, to fit your own personality and your
own inner necessity. But yours are not mine. This, I think,
is the prejudice that everybody gets hung up on. You talk
of conformist rules—I hate them myself—into which I
awkwardly forced the words in my first poem. Well, the
meter is conformist, but nothing else is—not even the
cadence. The poem, to anybody who believes without the
blinders of prejudice that a poem is alive when it speaks
with originality of language and force of feeling—the poem
sounds like me and nobody else!

All right. This is what I have done, to date. I am not
satisfied, either, because I want to find something new to
suit the whole wild area of my experience that I have not
yet given voice to. And I don't want my poems to be or to
look ragged—flung up onto the beach like driftwood—
which is the look so many have, and I don't mean the
iambic bunch. The problem, as I see it, is this: the
American poet writing today is between two snags, the first
being the academic New Criticism, which has resulted in
slick smooth banal "correct" performances, but has also
produced one genius, Robert Lowell, at least one; and the
second, the anti-academic reaction, such as the so-called
San Francisco jazz bunch, who generally spew their poems
out in ragged unformed inchoate blows, and of these
Ferlinghetti and Ginsberg are the only two who seem to be
aware of form at all, and who will probably do something in
this direction. Now where in hell do you put Jean Garrigue
whom you admire, and who writes pretty much in the
meters and even with the language sense of an English

Jacobean poet??? And she uses plenty of inversions, too. Don't tell me she has done anything new with the line, because she hasn't. What she has done was simply to swallow the New Critics, on whom she was weaned, and have the courage of her own sensibility to write as she *sees* and *feels*. What I am saying is this, in a nutshell: that's all that produces poetry, *seeing* and *feeling*—with that true unerring sensibility of the poet—and if we weren't living in a scientific mechanistic age of specialization, there wouldn't be so much emphasis on groups and ways of writing that exclude all other groups and ways of writing. Everybody is beating the tom-tom for his own special way and blinding himself to virtues in other ways because of sheer prejudice and nothing else. I have read of at least FIFTY poets each of whom was called the best or most important poet writing today. Somebody has to be wrong. All of them—Pound, Eliot, Graves, Rexroth, you—have singled out so-and-so and said, he or she is the best! Whose way is the only way?

Well, I'm getting long-winded. In fact, I just wrote an article demolishing Yvor Winters, whose way is the logical anti-associationist way, and who has made an ass of himself saying so. But in this article I cover the whole ground, I think, of literary specialists who are pretty blind, in the end, to other specialists, and all the famous ones of our age have been guilty of this. This doesn't help, I can tell you, the younger generations, but they will have to shift for themselves. If it's guidance they want, they've been born into the wrong time. They certainly won't get it. They can only become egotistical and prejudiced like their gods. Me, I'll follow my own little way and try to write honestly from my own experience, even if somebody else tells me it looks bad. If I discover anything about the line, it will be through making the effort myself, and nobody will be able to accuse me of imitation. If I don't, *tant pis.* Failure is not the terrible thing our American success-ridden culture makes it out to be. I am used to obscurity, which I'm beginning to think is the only way in which it is safe to work, after all. There are too many flags, too many drums, too many uniforms. Even individualism is conformity...

About *Paterson V.* I don't like it . I love *Paterson I* and *II,* especially *I.* But I think *V* is a falling away from the hard, clear directness, the immediacy of the scene and the man and the figures. I think it is a dissipation of the original impulse. It sounds like self-imitation. It doesn't rise anywhere to any kind of climax I can see. And it doesn't add a thing to what you've already said or done. Technically it disturbs me, because it looks ragged, which *Paterson I* and *II* do not. I am not speaking of *III* and *IV* because they were stolen from my library and I haven't read them in years. I seem to remember even there a falling off. But now you can tell me to go to hell for being a fool. No, I am wrong. I have just re-read it. I still don't like it, but I see that it doesn't look ragged, you have merely written a different kind of poem. *Paterson I* is really sensual, palpable, in the grain of the experience. *Paterson V* is an old man reminiscing. There's nothing wrong with the form here, and the language is loose and ready. Maybe this is what made me experience it as ragged, for *P.I* is dense, rich, involuted, rocky, ribbed, vaulted, flowing like a heavy river. I can see that *P. V* has remarkable things in it, but I still feel that it is a falling away of the lively experience.

O.K. We've said our piece. I hope you will not get sore, as I haven't gotten sore. I am more than responsive to suggestions, especially by poets like yourself, who have

really done something, suggestions about bringing more life
into the line, into the speech, of poetry. If you can help
me, perhaps that will he just the spur I need into self-
discovery! That's what I'm looking for!

My love to you and Floss. I leave July 7th. I'd be more
than willing to come out again, if you'll have me!

Hal

P.S. I have a nerve! I'm really nobody in the world of poets,
and you're famous & great—& listen to me talking like an
equal! There you have the limits of democracy. Let's hope
I'll really be president.

P.P.S. In this letter you single out "The Prince" but when
you first saw "Florence" in *Poetry*, you said "The Square" was
the best of the whole group. This is why I try to be equally
unmoved by either praise or blame!

William C. Wiliams M.D.
9 Ridge Road
Rutherford, N.J.
July 2/58

Dear Hal:

Ezra Pound was here, his party of 5, including Dorothy
his wife, spent Sunday night with us, Flossie on the couch
in the living room. They left yesterday afternoon. In this
exhausting weather thinking has not yet revived for me.

Thanks for your letter. If you can come out on the 4th

at the usual time we should be able to say something intelligent to each other by then. At least we can greet each other amicably by way of farewell. Poor Pound has had to withstand the whole country's hatred, we don't have to bear that Albatross about our necks.

Your comments about *Pat. 5* amount to just this in my mind, I am not today the man I was ten years ago. I am not for that reason alone dead. The theme has gone on into a higher bracket: that of the mind where all physical characteristics become ambivalent, take whatever characteristics the poet may assign to them.

Whatever worth *Pat. 5* may come to have in contrast to the other parts of the poem, I could not afford not to have written it.

Best
Bill

American Express
Florence, Italy
August 22, 1958

Dear Bill,

Back in Italy, and am I glad! I haven't had a sniffle, cough or sneeze since the moment I left New York! It is also significant that Jean Garrigue, who just wrote me from New York, is going through exactly the same symptoms of breakdown, allergy or whatever you want to call it. The rhythm, the pace, is so vastly different between Italy and the States, that the nervous system, once it is truly relaxed here, cannot take the sudden charge with which it is loaded in N.Y. No two ways about it. For better or for worse, the effect of N.Y. is to hop up a motor that, by nature, is meant to go slower, perhaps, than modern civilization allows it.

I've been reading your letters to me over the years, from the first one hailing my poem, "Warnings and Promises", to the last which is the hardest kick in the ass I've had to take heretofore. (Not the very last, as a matter of fact, which was an invitation to see you, my mother forwarded it to me after I left—but you had written it before we saw each other again and for some reason it didn't get to my N.Y. address till after I left.) I still haven't recovered really from that kick. In the end, you're right for one big reason— although wrong, I think, for all other reasons about my stuff. The big reason is your big contribution to poetry, which won't allow you to see or admit of any other kind as valid, namely, your lifelong devotion to the language of poetry as coming from colloquial, spoken, native speech as spoken in the American States. For this alone, as shown in your own work, your importance is undeniable. You're in the line of living classics—Catullus rather than Horace, Belli rather than Leopardi, Wordsworth rather than Coleridge, Shakespeare rather than Milton, Henry Miller rather than Henry James, Walt Whitman rather than Emerson, etc. By "living" I mean that kind of spoken speech of each age which sounds modern and alive in any age. Your continuous fight for it is like Lorenzo the Magnificent's fight to put the spoken Tuscan Italian on the literary map, after Dante chose it, rather than Latin, which everybody used for writing literature. I see it clearly and am all for it—but I also see clearly the greatness of the others, the scholar-poets of all ages (Villon and Shakespeare touch us more, with raw life clinging to the lines, but they are never sloppy or inadequate craftsmen for all that, and who would throw out Mallarmé or Verlaine just because Corbière is more colloquial?). I think from the beginning, to do what you had to do, you had to turn your back on Eliot, your contemporary, and pretend to yourself that he wasn't great. But the fact is, he *is* great, and this in no way diminishes you or vice versa. The sky is very large—it has room for all the stars, of different sizes and lustres. There is no competition in art—only different kinds of contributions. The mistake of each age is to be blind to this and to ignore or slight one artist in favor of another. But time like space is also large. Things right themselves in the end.

Well, I'm not making excuses, only describing my reactions. I think you slighted a lot of poems in my book because of the big blind spot about form and language, and if I am wrong, I'm only partially so. I'm actually working towards the freedom of the line and the word in it, and thanks to your harsh treatment (which I needed, I admit), I woke up to the fact that I've done enough in more or less traditional forms, and to satisfy my own drive—to be true to my own background—I have to kick over the traces and run wild again, not without control, as you say. But I have been reading Ginsberg and Kerouac, and all I can say is, you can have them, especially Kerouac. His book, *The Subterraneans*, is the most sloppily written drivel I've ever read and he makes Miller look like Henry James by comparison. He can't write. He can't create or develop characters, he can't focus his ideas and emotions, he can only run on and on in bop talk, and if that is good writing then I give up. Ginsberg seems to have more on the ball, but where is that control which differentiates art from automatic writing? They both talk very big and boost their egos in their work, naming each other as often as they can, like advertising soap or toothbrushes, they are good promotion men and their names have got around remarkably well, thanks to their gimmick of tying up with jazz and reading in night clubs. This is a slick stunt, and couldn't fail. But a lot of better poets and writers are being overlooked all the same because they haven't taken over American advertising methods. That's how I feel about it. I shall never believe that nothing succeeds like success. I'd rather fail than believe it. Jean Garrigue is a better writer than either of them will ever be, and she's leading a very quiet desperate life of comparative obscurity. She can't even get her new volume published—any more than I can get mine.

As for my volume, which you saw and didn't like, I've decided to drop it, anyway. If you're right, it can only harm me, even if it gets a good press. I'll get it back, and wait as long as I have to, to make a better book of it. I can perhaps divide it into more sections, leaving the more "formal" things at the end, representing earlier work. Who knows? I certainly am getting little or no guidance, cut off as I am. Anyway, *Sewanee Review* has just accepted a long poem of almost 200 lines about Spain, which I wrote there two years ago, and although the stanzas are more or less fixed, the language really runs, and it is really charged with experience. That's something.

I'm enclosing a few more or less recent ones for your comment. As for my remarks on *Paterson V*, I think that I was too concerned with licking my wounds to give you a really fair comment, I see that now in retrospect, although unconscious of this at the time. I still prefer the earlier sections, as I said, but thinking about it, about your going into the meditative rather than active mode, it made quite an impression on my unconscious, and some sections reached heights that even the earlier ones didn't contain. I for one would even like to see *Pat. VI*, going into a more spiritual dimension. If you can do this, the poem will take its place with the world's great classics. In *V* you go into the mind, the supremacy of the imagination. But if you really believe in that supreme being, that Unitarian God, as you and Floss told me, then the spiritual elements of your nature, which you have probably slighted all your life for more pragmatic and aesthetic considerations, ought now, for the first time, achieve their full expression. You are, after all, a great artist. You needn't go in for ouija boards or table-tapping—I am not suggesting a Yeatsy symbolism of the occult, etc., for this is alien to you—but it is in our American tradition to also have a transcendental attitude behind the pragmatic, as seen in Emily Dickinson and in Whitman. Express it! Only you—not Eliot, who is humanistic and European and oriental in a philosophizing, but magnificent way—can make that outer dimension a real experience by showing its existence in daily homely life, in all the objects of our familiarity. You have already dealt with death in *Journey to Love* and *The Desert Music*—now transcend it! Make the work of your old age rise to a pitch of exaltation that recaptures the spirit of living which was always, as it should be, identified by your youth with the physical sensations, and now that you have gone beyond them, you can celebrate the whole cycle of experience in a statement of faith! Make those Jersey dumps, those stinks and fragments and factories and rotting lots and backyards, those poverty-stricken squalid industry-ridden scenes live again and blaze with poetry! You have already given them to us in vivid detailed pictures, self-contained, the things in themselves. Now pull them all together; you are the mind that gave them, they did not give themselves. Go into the Mind that gave them to you, spoke through you, through your power, which after all is part of some greater Mind. It is a matter of finding one's true identity. Genius must never make the mistake of identifying itself solely with the ego, or it is lost. Humility and grandeur begin with understanding this.

Well, I've preached my sermon for the day. As for me, I'm making this also my aim. I'll dig into History, like a dog scratching for bones, to see what makes us live. And I'm not overlooking the saints, as well as the sinners. Remember Lao Tse and Tu Fu, men who saw the divine in trees and lakes and little simple scenes, whether they were drunk or sober. Their simplicity should not be underrated, and I'll make that my goal. We've let the complications of machines get under our skins, and we've gone too far from where we started, which can only end in confusion and disaster.

By the way, have you got an old photograph of yourself that you could send me? I meant to take one of you or both of us together or, in fact, all three of us, you, me and Floss, but never remembered to do so. I'd really like to have a picture; I'd put it into a small frame to keep it well. Meanwhile, wishing you health and good luck with everything. And what about your new work on prosody that you promised to send? I want to see it very much. It could probably help me out a lot.

110

Affectionately,
Harold

My love to Floss.

P.S. Please answer by airmail as it takes a month to get here & I will probably be going to Naples to teach in October.

I'd like to recommend a book that is simple, clear & impressive: *Ramana Maharshi & the Path of Self Knowledge* by Arthur Osborne (Rider, Ltd). Probably there's an American edition. A biography, but much more, as you will see.

William C. Williams M.D.
9 Ridge Road
Rutherford, N.J.
Sept. 2, 1958

Dear Hal:

Jean Garrigue is coming out tomorrow. I wish you could be here to join her, you can't do that from Florence. We'll think of you, meanwhile I'm glad you're where you want to be and look forward to seeing what'll do from this time forward. I'm interested in what you say of a possible *Pat. 6*, I never thought of going on into a still wider dimension and don't relish it. Well, we shall see. Meanwhile I never have pretended to be the distinguished person that you picture. Nuts with that. Let's go on being friends if you can stand it.

I like the poem you include in your letter. It is completely without inversions, which always pleases me, and the rhythmic flow of its language is unstilted, really very satisfactory to my ear. I like the whole set up of the verse as you have set it down, it bespeaks a subtle response to our language uninfluenced by teaching in the schools.

Let's not talk about the "variable foot" as long as you write in this way. Your defense of Eliot does you credit. I know he's an important poet but not one that can do you much good, just the opposite, you might just as well be following the Frenchman who is writing in Washington connected with the French embassy, I've forgotten his name. He also is out of touch with his age. Take your choice but, though you may be right in preferring the others, I can't see them.

This is just a short note since you give me a deadline to keep in touch with you while you are still in Florence. Tickled to death that [*Sewanee Review*] has taken your long poem but I think you are right in withholding your book. It needs work and growth of your thinking about your art. That is all I meant about the dictum that so hurt you. I was dissatisfied with the work I saw and could not permit it to be published with my approval.

Affectionately yours
Bill

Kerouac is not a poet, as you say, so I take no responsibility for him. I acknowledge mere automatic writing is nothing [but] thought may precede it and lead to some knowledge of construction, so we have to be alert to where it may lead.

Ginsberg is something else again, though mere dissolute language means also nothing. But if the construction of the phrase is under the influence of boring and tautologous dictates, the academe in short, a man must watch his step. Sometimes G. falls into that trap. Long lines or short make no difference.

Please note new address/
American Studies Center
Largo Ferrantina, 1
Naples, Italy
10 Sept. 58

Dear Bill,

Sending you a quick answer before I go down to Naples next week and get into the hectic life of teaching Italians English and ordering my own around writing in spare time. Thanks for the good words about my poem (I assume you are referring to my "Savonarola", since I sent two poems and you mentioned only one). Nevertheless, in spite of what you say, i.e. if I can write like that, no use talking about the "variable foot", I very much want to see what you write about it. A big problem with me is just that: measure. You say my "Savonarola" is very pleasing to your ear. Fine. But I haven't as yet discovered any single *measure*, variable foot, musical phrase or old iambics or trochaics or sprung rhythm or accentual or syllabic verse: not a single one I haven't tried, but I keep shifting around from one to another all my life, with varying success, and I want at last to light upon something. Long ago, I seemed to work best in a kind of free "playing by ear" sort of metric, close to prose stress, you might call it, or shifting accent. In any case, this is what variable foot must come down to—after all, it is impossible to go any further metrically than we have already done. After free verse and Pound's musical phrase, I suspect your variable foot can be only a refinement of the "musical phrase". It probably orders the look of it on the page, and taking the musical phrase as the metrical unit, allows a sort of free pattern to the line with a more organized look about it. Beyond that, there is nothing to discover, I think. And my "Savonarola" is merely a controlled free verse based on two or three or four prose stress accents to the line, nothing more. This gives it freedom of measure plus control, but at the same time I think it has too casual a look on the page. I also want something more tight to battle against. This kind of form offers no aesthetic resistance—there should be a control coming from the form itself.

Well, anyway I'm enclosing a couple of newer ones, one of which, "The Poisons of the World", may illustrate what I mean about controlling the form, giving it shape on the page. Yet this little one is too pat-looking altogether for my taste. It is a constant struggle—between the formless and too-fixed form. The one called "I Have Wasted My Life" is probably too loose altogether. This is why I think you've done so great a job in JOURNEY TO LOVE, where you've taken the maximum freedom of measure and given it a new kind of clean controlled form to the eye and ear. This is what I'd like to do, without sounding or looking like anybody else.

Have been re-reading JOURNEY TO LOVE. A great work—in "Asphodel, That Greeny Flower" you've already made some tremendous statements along the lines of which I was thinking you might expand for PATERSON VI. After all, in the "Coda", you feel naturally called upon to reach a sort of spiritual statement, which you do magnificently— "only the imagination is real" and "If a man die/it is because death/has first/possessed his imagination./But if he refuse death—" There you have it! You bring this into Paterson V anyway. But of course you know best what you can and what you should do. That important person I am making out of you—well, let's be friends anyway, *even if you are* that important person.

Have you seen Jean Garrigue? I wish I could have been there. As for my volume, yes I'm going to think about it a long time, but even if I do grow into something else, I should probably publish it after considerable deleting and changing poems around. It does represent a phase, a four-year period, and an experience, and whatever I do or don't do after it will represent another phase or period. I should be true to what I am at any given point.

Write soon and here's wishing all the best of health and everything to you and Floss!

Affectionately,
Hal

American Studies Center
Largo Ferrantina, 1
Naples, Italy
4 Oct./58

Dear Bill,

115

Finally got moved from Florence to Naples. It is no small thing to get lodgings in Naples that doesn't cost an eye. But I got an unbelievable deal—the first thing I saw—high on Posillipo, the hill over the Bay of Naples, like living in Amalfi or Capri, over the water—one room and bath, with a vast terrace in the sun, facing Vesuvius and Capri, all for 45 bucks a month. This involves paying extra for electric, concierge service, although he doesn't give any, etc. But I signed the contract with the American school which pays 150 bucks a month, so I can afford the luxury of living in Lotus Land. Posillipo—long a favorite resort of the ancient Greeks and Romans, who carved out caves from the igneous rock, making smooth sensuous golden grottoes everywhere, with houses and terraces to the sun and sea on the side of the cliff overlooking Naples, with palms and figs and eucalyptus and prickly pears and cedars and ferns and vines hanging over stone walls. Posillipo—I just found out the word means in Greek "pause from pain". What a wonderful word! It was de Nerval who wrote,

> *Dans la nuit du tombeau, toi qui m'as consolé,*
> *Rends-moi le Pausilippe et la mer d'Italie.*

Still, for me, there's a terrible cloud hanging over all this. Just the day before signing the contract to teach at the School, I was informed that there would be a "Security check" through Washington since the school comes partly under the United States Information Service jurisdiction, although in reality it is owned and operated by the Italo-American Association of Naples, a private organization. But the American bureaucracy will stick its finger into every pie. And what a finger! Always looking for communists and homosexuals and other terrible degenerates, so as to weed out the worst elements...the ones who think or feel or have ideals, we might say. I am no communist, nor was I ever one, officially, but I did sign many petitions that as a free American I had a free right to do, and I published a poem or two in radical papers. And as for my morals, although no better or worse than anybody else's, remember that disorderly conduct fine for a doorway episode, and *voilà*, a bad American. But I was told the "check up" takes about five months, so I signed anyway to live for a while in a way that I think I deserve, after so many years of hard luck. And even so, it's the first time I'm on a good salary in Italy, and it isn't even coming from the US government— yet they have to stick their big ugly Inquisitorial face—that bunch of cultural dinosaurs—into the picture and spoil it, take away the bread and the wine and everything but the insides of a man. Jefferson, Paine, Freneau, all the real Americans, must be very sour in their graves by now. Alex. Hamilton has won out after all. And the Fulbrights keep getting the dough. A bunch of bland unimaginative dopes.

I am keeping up with poetry by writing it, I don't see anybody else's, and feel cut off. But I'm enclosing some of the most recent. Let me know what you think. If you've done anything on the "variable foot", remember to send it to me. (Sailboats go by at my feet as I write this, flashing. And the sea licks at the caves.) It is all too good to be true. Curse all bureaucrats. When will man know how to live?

Affectionately,
Harold

Love to Floss.

Via Posillipo 38
Naples, Italy
12. XII. 58

Dear Bill,

Many thanks for *Paterson V* & the inscription to me. I had a
chance to re-read it—when you gave me the MS last spring
I was in no shape for anything, much less a judgment on
such a work. It seems to me above all no let-down in
technical or experimental achievement—very sure-footed,
as far as that goes—& there are some fine sections
throughout. I'm not nuts about all those letters you insert
that interrupt the poem proper. In the early *Paterson*
volumes there was some sort of relevance in such items as
Sam Patch, i.e. Americana. But why the letters from
Ginsberg & Josie (Herbst, I take it?) & Edward Dahlberg,
etc. Maybe I'm dense, but I just don't see it, so I can't say I
do. And they're so damn long, some of them. I find in re-
reading the poem, I skip the prose interpolations, & I'm
willing to bet they'll just fall into the back-alleys of literary
history one day & the poem will remain without 'em.

I've read it a 4th time—without the letters—only then
did it strike me fully & clearly—it grows and moves *without*
them damn letters that stop it up! The other prose bits are
OK.

I've also re-read Ginsberg & Corso & revised my opinion
on both. Corso is really talented after all, but he's so full of
shit about being original when he jist ain't. He's a local
copy of Apollinaire—why doesn't he quit talking about not

sounding like anybody but himself? He sounds just like Apollinaire who sounded a little better, like nobody else. But G.C., when he's not hopelessly bogged down in babbling, can turn out some memorable lines and rhythms, & sometimes he can even FEEL, which is something these days. As for the much publicized A.G., he certainly has a style of his own & a bitter but very funny humor, but he's too polemical—he is forcing poetry into sociology, & that never works. He's always beating some gong too loudly or beating his own chest, which makes the same hollow sound. I'm glad both of them are making a fuss, because it's needed. Only they'll have to be more serious about poetry—although they think they couldn't be more so.

As for me, Jonathan Williams is publishing my Belli translations (with your Preface) next month. Hurray! I've been laid up again for a month with the flu but getting stronger, & have written, I find, something like 25 poems during that month, some sort of record! They are all in a new vein, experimenting ceaselessly, & I find that I'm striking a style [in] them similar to the "Savonarola" poem I sent you. Did you get the others? When I hear from you, I'll try to send you a thick batch. I've got a wonderful title for...this new book I'm working on: CLASSIC FRIEZE IN A GARAGE. Do you like it? Don't tell anyone. The old world and the new, like my "Florence" poems—& I actually saw, on a street in Naples, the incredible juxtaposition—in an old garage where mechanics were welding & greasing & blow-torching cars, two huge classic friezes, hardly the worse for wear, stood proudly and majestically over the Fiats, the mechanics—the gasoline!

The best of the Christmas & New Year's Season to you both.

Ever,
Hal

P.S. I still want to know how your "variable foot" develops
anything NOT in the "musical phrase"?!?

W . C . Williams M. D.
9 Ridge Road
Rutherford, N.J.
Dec. 17, 1958

Dear Hal:

A damned good title. Mum's the word. But you tell us
nothing of your personal affairs, did you get the new
teaching job and are you able to keep it indefinitely?
Loosen up. I see that your address is still Naples so that I
am permitted to infer that your patron still sticks to you
and perhaps the government has not interfered.

That Jonathan Williams is going to bring out the Belli
translations is good news, so we'll see them at last. As to
my inclusion of the letters in *Pat.* 5 and previously, it was
perhaps questionable in such a poem, but I didn't know
how else to get the current contemporary feeling and the
essential idiomatic similarity between all elements of the
American idiom. They are of one piece, even Pound admits
that, and they're not governed by the classic divisions of
English composition. The letters as they were written
come closer to my verse, in the mode I adopt, and so form a
uniform pattern. They were to my feeling part of the

whole.

In addition prose and verse go together for me for the relief they bring to the writer and reader. It emphasizes the elevation of the verse—tho of course Dante cannot have thought so, but he had the *Vita Nuova* to fall back on.

I think I told you that I have had another stroke which at 75 is serious business. Wish me luck, I am still able to get about. In fact I have a new play, *Many Loves*, coming out in 4 days. Hope it goes through. I wish the producers the best of luck. My program has to be drastically restricted otherwise. Not much fun any more.

I'll have to quit now, Merry Christmas and a Happy New Year. A book on the conversation of my mother has been announced for June.

Take care of yourself

Bill

Via Posillipo 38
(Grottaromana)
Naples, Italy
11.1.59

Dear Bill,

It was good to hear from you again after so long but not so good to know about the new stroke. You have to take it easy, no doubt, but I'm sure you'll be all right again soon. You've got my best wishes for you.

Yes, I got the job here and have been working but all the same there is an "investigation" being made in

Washington, and I expect some time around March to feel the sharp end of the axe, but till then I'm earning money. My patron is a great man and always sticks by me, and offers help the first moment my means of support are withdrawn. I wish you two could know each other.

Thanks for the explanation of why you use the prose sections in *Pat. V*. You're no doubt right and my own thinking is probably governed by a more rigid concept of structure in poetry—it is just that, for experiment, I tried reading the poem SKIPPING the prose, & found to my surprise & pleasure that the poetry gained in intensity rather than the other way round. "... they're not governed by the classic divisions of English composition," you say. Well, O.K., but that in itself can be good or bad, depending on the use you make of it. In any case, I hope to see a *Pat. VI*, more like a Coda to the whole work, with maybe a deeper dimension of experience??—a *lifting* into the rare plain song of the great man who has come a long way & knows how to close with dignity & depth—& may all the others envy you for the ground you broke & the honesty with which you see & write ("deeper dimension": already in *Desert Music*.)

I have written about 35 or 40 poems in the last three months—the new book—& am sending you a big batch next week. Hope you like 'em. Meanwhile, I have no idea of what to do about the other volume you saw, since there are many poems that should appear in book form. I confess that being so far from the States and from friends I'm at a loss for anything that concerns publication. Work has piled up and I haven't sent anything out. But the Belli book ought to kick up a real fuss, if not a storm! And may the damn fools enjoy their self-righteous hypocrisies!

Let me know how you are from time to time. My

warmest wishes for a good New Year to you & Floss.

God bless!
Hal

9 Ridge Road
Rutherford, N.J.
Jan. 30/59

Dear Hal:

Something has come over you, these are the best you have ever sent me—I haven't yet finished reading them but the first 2 or 3 in this batch are superb. All sense of straining has in these three poems disappeared from your writing and your control of the language has blossomed like a flower, a sense of ease has taken possession of you which I have never before seen in your work. I'll get Floss to read me more just as soon as she can be captured. I am delighted to be able to write in this way, it makes me as happy as I hope it makes you.

(2 days later)

My first impression has been confirmed, Floss read the poems to me and she enjoyed them as much as I did, especially the first, the *Piccolo Paradiso*, that will stand up anywhere among the best poems of our times. We have marked also "Power," "Neapolitan Fortress," "Polemical Monologue," "The Oil Refinery," and "Masaccio," "Libeccio," "Color Scheme," "Winter Scene" and "Polemic

I."

You have breached a new lead, shown a new power over the language which makes theories of composition so much blah—save that they open the artist's eyes to what is going on about him and free him to record unchecked by academic rules. Your freedom in the measure is worth all the rest to me.

I hope your case is going well. The best of luck. Regards from Floss.

Devotedly yours
Bill

Via Posillipo 32
(Grottaromana)
Naples, Italy
1.III.59

Dear Bill,

Many thanks for the praise. It gave me a lift. I thought you'd like them. They are the poems that will make up the third volume, *Classic Frieze in a Garage*, which I ought to get together soon. The second volume, which you didn't like on the whole, I've edited severely, & although I've had to keep *some* of the poems you hated, it's a strong book & I'll try to get it printed for no other reason than that it's a stage along the way. But the current poems, which open out to the reader & knock him on the head, I hope, are very probably the result, in part, of that fight we had last summer. Thank you for winning. It loosened me up &

brought me in touch again with my own language & my own way of making sounds or noises in my own measures, for better or worse. I don't think I'll ever go back to the traditional measures again, although they taught me to respect language, something which the noisy overpublicized "beat" boys have not yet learned. And after all, the "beat" generation is my own, those are my experiences, too, but they write about all the mess of the Forties & Fifties from the pulpit or the proscenium, the *outside*, when after all true poetry begins from the inside; I think I'm finding my voice, & I want to explore the inner processes of my relation to myself & society—but self *always* comes first. Hence, "Piccolo Paradiso" is a beat poem, & so is "Masaccio" & "Winter Scene," & even "Polemic I." You can't talk about Buddha from the soapbox as if he were Karl Marx. This is what I feel when I read Ginsberg.

Could you do anything about letting Rosenthal see the poems I sent you & perhaps he'd like some for *The Nation?* I'm so sick of being ignored. How long can I go on being a poet's poet? Jean Garrigue was positively sent by "Masaccio," but she hasn't seen the others yet.

I've had a lull for a few weeks, no writing, but soon I'll be getting along with my nearly finished *Italian Journal*, & then there's a chance of a studio in Paris, gratis, which I'm ready to grab. If we don't go and fight the Russians & blow up the earth altogether, things ought to be looking up from now on. In the end, we're all egocentric, so let's hope spring will thaw the savage hearts of even our political beasts.

I've written a "Polemic III," by the way, calling God to account for the mess of Creation, & I'll send it along with some others soon. Have poems coming out in *Sewanee*,

Poetry & *Paris Review* & sending some to Daisy Alden for a new number of *Folder*. Do you know of it? Would appreciate hearing of any good mags that might get my work seen. I've sent most of the new ones to Rago at *Poetry* but he's pissed off at me for a critical letter I sent last year saying what lousy taste *Poetry* had been showing recently, so maybe he won't take kindly to my new work.

Keep well, for God's sake, & as always I'd like to hear how you are, what you're publishing, etc. No *Paterson VI?* I still think there's a great poem in your subconscious knocking at the gates to be let out!

My best as ever, to you and Floss!

Hal

Jonathan Williams hasn't answered me in months, so I don't know what's happening to my forthcoming Belli book!

Via Posillipo 38
(Grottaromana)
Naples, Italy
6.IV.59

Dear Bill,

Just a brief one to ask how you are—haven't heard from you although I sent you a letter a while back. Hope all goes well. I am leaving Italy in May for—Paris! Someone I know has been kind enough to offer me a studio there, rent-free, and all I have to do is see that I have enough money to eat on, which I hope my Armenian friend will put up. Although he hasn't answered any letters now in months. PARIS! ! ! To *live* there! ! What I have always wanted. It's amazing how much one can do on no money at all—let's hope it keeps up. I can safely say, if my work hasn't rewarded me in prizes, fellowships, or wide recognition, it has supported me, more or less, in the last five years in Europe—through people who have money *and* taste *and* the desire to help, no matter how little. At least, it's kept me in Europe.

Speaking of my work, have you had a chance to see M.L. Rosenthal & show him any of the recent stuff? Should I just send some to him for *The Nation*, as I would anywhere else, cold? I just thought he might get enthusiastic enough to do something... ho hum. *That* is another story. And by the way, my usual lousy luck in "career" is still with me: Jonathan Williams was supposed to publish my Belli book in January. Not only has he not done it yet, but now for some mysterious reason does not even answer my letters; four months of silence! On the other hand, there have been lots of acceptances: POETRY (they took "Winter Scene", "Color & Sound" & one you haven't seen, but turned down "Piccolo Paradiso" & "Masaccio"); PARIS REVIEW; SEWANEE REVIEW (long poem I told you about) and more recently FOLDER: they took "Polemic III" which you haven't seen, attacking anthropomorphic God-with-long-beard.

Have been reading Pound's prose; it comes as a shock that he not only admired Mussolini (there was no doubt something to admire in the early man) but also HITLER

AND FATHER COUGHLIN. The only one he doesn't
mention is Mosley, and that was probably because he was
English. Another shock: he feels close to the Catholic
Church of Rome, & in one place says he would make "a
good Catholic" if they let him choose his own saints...How
perverse can a man get? His attitude to the Jews is
everywhere irrational. He doesn't make a single sensible
statement that would hold up reasonably in his emotional
attacks on them—no better than his admired Hitler.

If you reply by AIR MAIL, your letter will get here
before May 1st. If not, I will in the future be at the
following address:

c/o Laurin
9 Rue Thiers
Boulogne-sur-Seine
Seine (Paris) France

Wishing you & Floss all my warmest (I thought of her
rhubarb pie the other day as I sat looking at the
Mediterranean & Vesuvius—& the pie WAS serious
competition!!)

Hal

9 Ridge Road
Rutherford, N. J.
[April 13, 1959]

Dear Hal:

You never told whether or not you are still hanging onto your job and will it be good for next year also. I note the Paris address, thank you, I'll keep it in my files.

Nothing I can do about Jonathan Williams' failure to print the Belli translations—but I congratulate you on your successes with the other magazines. Send Rosenthal some poems for *The Nation*. If they are not too long I am sure he'll print some of them—but I never see him any more since I have had to withdraw from the active field due to my recent, last September stroke. Last winter was a hard time for me, I don't know how I survived it and kept going. It was a real hell for me.

One of the things that kept me up was a promise by Dave McDowell to print my book on my mother to appear on June 1. I have just seen the page proofs—don't expect too much from it, nothing goes well for me these days, but I can't afford to complain. This is further evidence of my maladroitness that I have begun my letter on the wrong side of the sheet. I'll have to stop here and go to the proper side which will be easier for you to read—perhaps.

(continued) As I was saying when I discovered the error I have made—[I can't] quit for that would hog-tie me completely, my friends can't afford to wait indefinitely for me. I was talking of the book Dave has promised to bring out June 1. It will not be a job that I can be proud of, too many false starts until I had to let it go, just, as it stands.

To keep myself busy I have been writing a book from day to day called PICTURES FROM BRUEGHEL, poems. I hope they are poems describing each painting as I studied it (from excellent color prints) item by item, 12 in all. I really slaved over this, doing them at times over and over—to keep myself busy those heartbreaking January and

February days. Now it is finished, 12 one page poems. I am thinking of sending them for her approval to Marguerite Caetani. If she turns them down I'll try elsewhere.

Glad you attempted to read Pound's *Cantos*. They are for the most part too much for me as my mind has slowed up with age—and I agree with you, ever since the Mussolini and Hitler incidents, to say nothing of what happened in Spain, the whole Franco incident, I have not been able to swallow him except as a poet and an old friend.

The Jews as a class are not congenial to me—but that's mainly of their own choosing. Right now I have a middle aged Jew named Theodore Harris who is furiously composing an opera on a libretto on the theme of Geo. Washington! You'll be hearing more of that later.

Got to quit now, I'm weary. Hope your Armenian friend has not finally gone back on you. Best from Floss— her new roses are just being planted.

Kiss Paris on the wrist for me. Have a good time there.

Yours
Bill

Via Posillipo 38
(Grottaromana)
Naples, Italy
20/IV/59

Dear Bill,

Many thanks for your quick reply. I had no idea that you were so ill this last winter & I am relieved you pulled through. In any case the poems on Brueghel sound good from your mere mention of them. The Princess Caetani is as capricious in her taste as she is in her generosity, so don't expect much. Yes, I'll send some to Rosenthal at *The Nation*—at least, my stuff is coming out, but only like the iceberg, a small part protruding above the surface.

Jonathan Williams just conked out of our correspondence so I don't know what's happening. I have a contract or rather a gentleman's written agreement with him, for what it's worth.

As for Pound, some day I'd like to write a book or an article, at least, about him, a *sottisier* that should help deflate his image, now an icon to the very young, & a very dangerous one. As poet he is one thing, but remember he has written much prose, much of it about as sensitive, socially, as Hitler, & able to lead to similar effects. You say, "The Jews as a class are not congenial to me," but Pound like a mad dog attributes usury AND Christianity to them, & blames them, as Hitler did, for society's ills. It seems to me that exterminating 6 million of them has not improved things. As for me, substitute "human beings" for "Jews" in your statement, & there's my attitude. What's all this fuss about the Jews but a habit? After all, Pound fumes at the mouth even more violently about the English & the Americans. And just take a little trip to modern Germany & see whether you'd prefer the Germans to the Jews, if you had to make a choice. God knows, the Italians are impossible enough, money-mad, materialistic, superficial, noisy, pushy, inconsiderate, etc. BUT I find them the easiest to get along with in Europe, so far. It's the human race, Jews & all! A plague on it, it's a disease & it may well die of self-poisoning! The antidote—small doses of individuals, once daily. Pound gets under the skin, a rash on the surface. The *Cantos* are certainly a blob—but each age gets the rulers and poets it deserves, & he's representative of this one. But I don't think those long crazy economic tracts filled with hate & "unacknowledged legislator" vindictiveness will stand up for long. The next generation, or the one after, having swallowed it, won't pass it on.

Well, my Armenian will come across—*there's* a great guy—& I'll write frorn Paree! Take care.

Best to you & Floss,
Hal

42 Rue St. Louis En L' Ile
c/o Laurin
Paris 4, France
24.7.59

Dear Bill,

Two months in Paris, so far, & just beginning to come down out of the clouds. What a difference! After that burst of short poems in Naples, I fell asleep for several months & like to of drowned! Here there's all the excitement there ever was in the Twenties, I'm sure of it. Don't let anyone tell you different. Thanks to you & Pound, & a few later comers, poetry is really looking up again in this generation & the next. The Americans I meet are alive, thank God, not the ugly tourist-type. Mebbe there are too many beards & dirty feet in sandals, but that's all to the good. You've busted up the academic stranglehold on my generation of the last twenty years. It took me a long time to shake it off—& not the least of the credit goes to you & those hard talks we had last year in Rutherford. But bless you, you're a poetry doctor, too! And although the operation was painful, & I kicked against the scalpel, I mended afterwards, & no scars! It's true. I'm coming out. Whatever I had that wasn't of the school-sort is returning. I'll send you my new things when I can. Meanwhile, met Corso here, & we practically fell into each other's arms, like brothers. Another East Side kid! He's really a natural, & I envy him his lack of schooling! In any case, he liked my stuff a lot & asked me to appear with him in a very small pamphlet of one poem each, but it will circulate in the States, & I like being associated with the Beatniks, since I'm really one, after all, it's the experience of my generation, I went thru it all, & then some. He's lucky he didn't go thru the moaning & whining of the Depression when I was only a little kid, but saw home relief investigators in the house eyeing me like another mouth Franklin D. had to feed.

The Belli book has been taken over & backed by the Eighth Street bookshop, that is now behind Jonathan Williams, & it looks good for Fall publication. They're supposed to send me a contract, & then all will be well. Meanwhile, my second volume, that you saw & snarled at last year, I have edited ferociously & will try to publish, although it ain't Beat, but it's mine & I might as well get it off my chest, the time lag in publishing ain't my fault. And then after that, it's the new look for me!

Hope you're doing well, you & Floss, & that you're working well too. I hear a lot these days about your book on measure, the Beats talk about it, & I'd like to see it if it's out. Let me know how you are. And if you know anybody here that should see me, or anybody coming over, please put us in touch. The more the merrier. The American Renaissance is real. I want to be around Americans now. And I'm thinking of a return, mebbe for good, next year. All the best to you both.

Hal

42 Rue St. Louis En L'Ile
Paris 4, France
16/III/60

Dear Bill,

How have you been?? My last two letters are still unanswered. I don't think it has anything to do with your being pissed off, for some reason, at me? I can't think of any reason why. In any case, I'm writing to tell you that finally the Belli translations were published last week in New York by Jonathan Williams. And Alberto Moravia will send you the 100 slips of paper for your signature which will be inserted in each of 100 copies of the deluxe edition. I guess Jon. Wms has explained all this to you.

How the hell are ya? Hope you find time to write to an old friend. My life in Paris has been, funnily enough, lonely. It's a cold city in more ways than one, there are too many artists and would-be's, and the competition that we associate with manufacturers, chain stores and oil comp- anies seems to be characteristic of poets and painters here, too. I don't like it, I never liked it. I can't think of writing poetry "in competition" with anyone else. To me it has always been a private struggle to get my own life down on paper in the most effective way—& perhaps to my own detriment, I've been too much the lone wolf among what turns out to be, after all, a wolfpack. Fangs are bared at my approach, even the wolves turn against me.

But all that is just shit to me. I've had some good luck recently, which you'll be glad to hear. Paul Carroll, editor of *Big Table*, has taken some poems and probably an essay, in which I credit you with being the main influence on all the most important work being done by Beatniks and rebels. This will be in THE NEW AMERICAN POETS ISSUE NO 4 of BT. After a raving letter, two in fact, from Carroll about my recent poems, saying I'm one of the best, the other editors sent back a large batch of poems, altho he specifically requested them to represent me by "a large hunk of work". I don't know why he's only taken two poems so far after working himself up to such enthusiasm about me. I sometimes think I have powerful enemies among the wolfpack. I have seen how they turn against one, against you, the very ones who *owe* you most. I can never do this. I acknowledge in my essay the tremendous influence you exerted over me in those summer days at Rutherford in 1958, before I returned to Europe. I can't stand treachery, least of all literary treachery. And will compromise myself for nobody, for no ends. This means the fight will be and is against overwhelming odds. Or am I raving? Do I make sense? Or am I preaching?? Anyway, I've said it.

The poems I have done this year are free and stylistically something new, I think. Anyway, they came from a necessity to break up the "authority" pattern prevalent in non-Beat poetry—altho I can't call mine "Beat" either. I don't know what to call it—just poetry.

I hope this letter finds you & Floss in the pink, & that you'll answer finally, even if [just] a few words. Here I've seen much of Corso, Burroughs, & some others—they are certainly "famous", the way movie stars are, or jazzmen. I don't think I'll ever achieve that. I'm not at all sure I want to. I just want to say my piece & have a few people I admire recognize it.

Au revoir,
Hal

9 Ridge Road
Rutherford, N.J.
April 25, 1960

Dear Harold:

I hasten to answer you, there is so much to tell you, and I am not up to it as I was formerly when an 8 page letter was no stunt at all for me as it is now. It would take at least ten pages to tell you how much I think of you now—my appreciation of the importance of the work you are doing is right in the front of my head.

At this moment I received a telephone call from Theodore Harris, a composer who is doing an opera on a score for which I did the libretto 12 years ago. If we think we have troubles they fade to nothing when faced with the troubles musical composers are faced by. Harris is a man of 46. He's good, he's having a hell of a time getting a hearing. Put his name prominently on your calendar.

I've received recently about 50 signed or I mean autographed cards for your Belli translations which Jonathan Williams is bringing out shortly. Have they been missent to me by someone in Italy because of the identity of the surname?

No harm done. I'll keep them for him until I get a clearer notion of what I am to do with the cards.

But the thing that remains for me to do is assure you of my loyalty to you. I believe in your intellectual honesty. And also in what you are doing—but if you will send a further sample of your most recent work it would be welcomed by me. I am far from being moved by what the so-called "Beatnik" poets are doing. The structure of the line cannot be elided. It goes deeper than what most of them are up to. No amount of behavioristic posturing does anything more for me than make me smile. The French and no doubt the Italians have far surpassed that long since.

Picasso and the surrealist painters have left the poets among us nailed to the mast. The French, Cocteau, have returned if not to Mallarmé to the neo-classicism of their academicism. The English with the rejection of T.S. Eliot don't know where to turn. None of them knows the meaning of, the hope of, the variable foot which I pointed out in our famous conversation on our back lawn, 2 years ago. A name that is just coming to be known is that of a poet and essayist named Mary Ellen Solt whose essays you will hear of shortly.

Mary Ellen Solt puts the Beatniks to shame because she has thought the thing through and come up with the variable foot as even the basis of the surviving excellence of Ezra Pound's line. It goes clean back to Walt Whitman, though he did not carry it half far enough. It remains for us to carry on the significance of it if we can think it through and not get stuck with our poor Beatniks.

They have missed the turn. It hinges in the English language on the American idiom from which they are barred by their prejudice against us, and ours against them. The VARIABLE FOOT in any language is the modern variant which would free us all. I wish I could make you see that it is your future in which the Beatniks would gladly join you if they had brains enough. Ah well, we may have to leave it to Ellen Solt and her generation. It's a pity that I have to go on alone.

Bill

42 Rue St. Louis En L'lle
Paris 4 France
1.VI.60

Dear Bill,

What a treat to hear from you again after such a long time! I was startled to see that over a month had rolled by & I had not answered your packed & stimulating letter—for several reasons. I was ending one affair & beginning another, with a young unhappily married American girl, & now it looks like the coast is clearing & we will go to Rome together in two weeks. I look forward to this with a mad kind of joy. Also, I was finishing the last sections of a travel book—hitch-hike I once took—through Italy.

It makes me more happy than I can say that your "appreciation of the work you are doing is right in front of my head". I have been fortunately kept alive this last year and probably the next by my wonderful patron & so I have written a great deal and am trying hard to hack out the problems you touched upon in your letter. I will try to send on some more recent stuff. I think you will probably know of a new magazine, BETWEEN WORLDS, edited by Gilbert Neiman, a friend of Henry Miller's, in Puerto Rico and subsidized, I hear, by the Ford Foundation. He took 8 poems of mine—all I sent—for the first number, and it is a good sample of how my style is evolving. I will send you other poems, and hope you see the mag. It should be out by now. I am still trying to find out what the difference is between your *variable foot* & Pound's *musical phrase*. Is it the same thing? Does the measure rely solely on the ear, as if playing by ear, from natural speech/prose rhythms? How is it measured? I know I play by ear—I've chucked out forever those iambics that made your blood boil when you opened my second volume two years ago. As I say, I had to do it that way. I learn slowly and only from my own experience. I want so goddam much to understand just what you mean when you say "I wish I could make you see that it is your future (the variable foot) in which the Beatniks would gladly join you if they had brains enough. Ah well, we may have to leave it to Ellen Solt and her generation. It's a pity that I have to go on alone." Now what has happened to all those other poets of my generation whom you used to praise precisely because they seemed to have absorbed your message about language and measure? What about Blackburn (to me a tiresome poet because, outside of his Provençal translations, he has nothing to say)? Olson (again tiresome because ponderous, pachydermous, completely earless, an imitator, not a fresh start, a big ounce of Pound)? Creeley, Levertov?? And erstwhile Ignatow? All those people you said were carrying on with the v. foot or doing something fresh? Why do you say you have to go on alone?

As for the Beatniks, I agree with you completely when you say "...no amount of behavioristic posturing does anything more for me than make me smile. The French and no doubt the Italians have far surpassed that long since". How right you are! But their value lies in a kind of shock treatment they gave the cataleptic American poetry of the Forties—& I must admit that I too was walking around America in a catatonic state then, too hurt & hungry & confused & miserable to do more than occasionally cry out in bitterness and impotent rage every now and then, but for the most part sunk in iambic despair, stuck like a fly in amber, going to pieces in pentameter verse! What a period! What a youth! From the Depression to the War, my puberty and adolescence was one muddy quagmire of sick grief from which I thought I would never be able to raise my head. I am not sorry for anything that happened, I am even glad of it now. It had to be. But when in the Fifties the so-called Beatniks burst out with an expression of rage, a scream of anger and accusation, I recognized that my generation had finally expressed itself. All that I had gone through was at last made public in HOWL. It was not great poetry nor measured poetry, but it was *poetry* in the true sense because it rebelled successfully against the strangling influences of conformity & authority that the universities had straitjacketed it with. I didn't *like* HOWL, I didn't think it would bear up under any kind of literary analysis. But it made despair articulate, it broke thru the sound-barrier of academic rule, and had a living voice. It was a spoken truth. It will always have a place, like the *Journal of Albion Moonlight*, as a record of the human psyche during one decade. As for the other Beatniks, or Ginsberg himself as he is now, most of them still have a driving vitality which is so much needed in American verse. They are influenced by Surrealism and so on, as you say, and perhaps it was all done much better, and you are right when you say, "They have missed the turn. It hinges in the English language on the American idiom from which they are barred by their prejudice against us and ours against them". Yet, when I look at your statement real close, I begin to wonder how you can say the second part of it—for what Kerouac, Ginsberg, Corso & Burroughs have done is precisely to restore spoken speech, the *American* speech, to literature after you & Pound had been sidestepped for Eliot, i.e. the Beatniks *returned* to you & Pound & thus swung the pendulum away from Eliot & the "New Criticism". As for their "posturing", I agree. Success, the kind that movie stars get, has not been too good for them. But I'd blame this more on the American society that always wins in the end against the artist who rebels against it, because with recognition and money America swallows up its rebels and makes it tough for them to sustain what in their obscurity they could nurture: their sincerity. Once recognized by television cameras and the slick magazines, the original need for expression turns into a pose, a posture. But their work is done; and as a fashion, give them another year or two & they will be ceding their place to another fashion.

"But the thing that remains for me to do is to assure you of my loyalty to you. I believe in your intellectual honesty. And also in what you are doing—" Bill, this moves me more than I can say. If such feelings are still alive in the world

between two humans, even though we are on the much
forecast brink of total devastation, & all our emotions, feelings and thoughts are already shaking and breaking apart,
then I for one continue to have faith in individuals. We are
crying across vast canyons now. Soon the canyons themselves will be swallowed up. But I believe in the survival of
the poem, the word, even when matter itself goes.

My best to you & Floss—

Hal

P.S. After June 15: 49 Via dell Anima, Rome, Italy.
P.P.S. I'm enclosing my poem "Classic Frieze In A Garage".

William Carlos Williams
9 Ridge Road
Rutherford, N.J.
June 13, 1960

Dear Hal:

That's better, in fact these poems headed by "Classic
Frieze in a Garage" are the best I have seen of yours since
the very beginning. I don't mind telling you I was
beginning to think you were lost to me forever. It broke
my heart because I counted on you as being the one guy
who would carry the battle without flagging deep into the
enemy territory. I thought you were beginning to weaken
at last, beginning to give ground before the onslaught of
the iambic pentameter, blank verse in short, the academy—

that our famous garden meeting when we both got hot under the collar had done no good.

But I was wrong, *Gott sei dank.* The American idiom won out in the end—or is winning out in the end. This poem is the sign of it. The whole make up of this poem, what it says in the text of it, insures that I was only fearful that you yourself might not be convinced that the minute construction of the lines following your native idiom might have escaped you.

I should have had more confidence in you perhaps but these matters are so important to me, involving the whole position of what I am, that I couldn't take a chance on being misunderstood without a fight.

Your whole letter built up to this poem as a convincing climax. I'm glad you have made connection with Mary Ellen Solt in your own generation. She is about to release an essay [in] midsummer which I have hopes [for] in carrying the ball; it will be given in a lecture at Indiana University. The girl is giving herself to it wholeheartedly. She's a devotee, I hope only that is not over training or writing for the event, but she's a solidly built individual with iron nerves and a flaming spirit. She'll make good, she spent the night under our roof, has been to Italy and Oxford and knows what it's all about, a fighter.

Which is more than the Beatniks do, although they have accidentally hit on the right idea. (At this moment I received a phonecall from my composer who has written an opera but has not got the money to produce it.)

Good luck to you with the girl, may she be all you expect of her.

Sincerely devotedly yours
Bill

William Carlos Williams
9 Ridge Road
Rutherford, N.J.
Aug. 26/60

Continuing what I was saying in the garden. Greetings.

THE AMERICAN IDIOM

The American idiom is the language we speak in the
United States. It is characterized by certain differences
from the language used among cultured Englishmen, being
completely free from all influences which can be summed
up as having to do with "the Establishment". This, pared to
essentials, is the language which governed Walt Whitman
in his choice of words. It constituted a revolution in the
language. (In France only Paul Fort recognized what had
happened about him to negate the *académie*.)

The language had been deracinated in this country but
the English tongue was a tough customer with roots bedded
in a tradition of far-reaching cultural power. Every nursery
rhyme gave it a firmer grip on the tradition and there were
always those interested in keeping their firm hold upon it.

Every high school in America is duty bound to preserve
the English language as a point of honor, a requirement of
its curriculum. To fail in ENGLISH is unthinkable!

Ignoring the supreme masters of English composition
and thinking to go beyond them along the same paths
impugns a man's loyalty if not his good sense. In fact it has
been baldly stated in the highest circles and believed that
there is no American language at all, so low have we fallen
in defense of our speech.

The result is a new and unheralded language which has grown stronger by osmosis, we are asked to believe, but actually by the power of those Whitmans among us who were driven to take a chance by their fellows and the pride of an emerging race, its own. The American idiom had been driven into a secondary place by our scholars, those rats that had abandoned it to seek salvage elsewhere in safer places. No one can blame them, no one can say that we shall survive to plant our genes in another world.

We must go forward, uncertainly it may be, but courageously as we may. Be assured that measure in mathematics as in verse is inescapable, so to the fixed foot of the ancient line including the Elizabethans we must have a reply: it is the variable foot which we are beginning to discover after Whitman's advent.

"The Establishment," fixed in its commitments, has arrived at its last stand: the iambic pentameter, blank verse, the verse of Shakespeare and Marlowe, which give it its prestige. A full stop. Until we can go beyond that, "the Establishment" has an edge on us.

Whitman lived in the nineteenth century but he, it must be acknowledged, proceeded instinctively by rule of thumb and a tough head, correctly, in the construction of his verses. He knew nothing of the importance of what he had stumbled on, unconscious of the concept of the variable foot. This new notion of time which we were approaching, leading to the work of Curie and the atom bomb, and other NEW concepts, has been pregnant with far reaching consequences.

We were asleep to the tremendous responsibilities as poets, and as writers generally, that were opening up to us. Our poets especially are asleep from the neck [up]—only the Russians with their state control of letters are stupider than we. And still we follow the English and teach it to our unsuspecting children.

William Carlos Williams

49 Via S. Maria dell' Anima
Int. 8, Rome, Italy
8/IX/60

Dear Bill,

Many thanks for THE AMERICAN IDIOM which reminded me, also, that I owed you a letter. The move from Paris to Rome has been more complicated, in many sudden & unforeseen ways, than I had expected: loss of one girl, one Paris apartment, & one stimulating environment. So I just couldn't get around to writing any letters, much less poems, in the last two months. The girl didn't come to Rome; instead she vamped a Paris editor & is having her first book of poems out soon. Anyway, I don't begrudge her. She's a good poet, I woke her up, she writes me warm letters, & anyway her husband came back! As for THE AMERICAN IDIOM, it's a snappy broadsheet & of course I go along with it, but somehow it seems to me unfinished, as if you had only gotten started. I have the feeling that there is more to say, to give out to the reader, to the world, that you have left unsaid—about poetry, something specific; I always feel that you mention the variable foot, whetting my appetite, but don't give your own specific definition. Of course, it's all in your poems & all you have to say is, read

146

them! But on one question you've never answered me (or the reader, for all I know): how does the variable foot differ, or develop from, the musical phrase? Are they synonymous? Anyway, it's good to do these broadsides.

Your last letter about my poem, "Classic Frieze in a Garage", made me very happy. I'm going on now, for the rest of my life, experimenting. That fuckin' iambic pentameter, as far as I'm concerned, is purged out of my system like a dose of poison from the Forties—& anyway, I was a real victim of the worst kind of environment, the timid fearful milieu of that time when poets agreed with Auden that "poetry makes nothing happen". I can't help it if I was a youth growing up in New York then. I was also a rebel, but almost nobody would publish my resistance poems, & for a few years I too fell into the lockstep. But depression & war are not bound to make a tender spirit happy; it was a slow suicide at best. In the Fifties I snapped out of it by taking a boat for Europe. Believe it or not, our garden talk—thanks to your experience, kindness & stubbornness—was a major moment. Maybe for both of us, as it made you even surer of your point. And for me, it snapped me back, this time for good, to live language & live cadence.

Have you seen the mag BETWEEN WORLDS? I have eight poems in it. Also BIG TABLE 4. I'm pretty much out of touch here & want to get back to Paris & am thinking of return to USA in a year or so, California, no doubt. If you think Mary Ellen Solt would like a correspondence with me, I'd be very glad if you gave her my address. Perhaps we could come up with something interesting together. I'll be here for another month or so, & will drop you a line as to my new whereabouts when I know what it is myself. I'm

sending a few poems to you under separate cover. Always
anxious to hear from you. But you better send next letter
AIRMAIL as it takes two or 3 weeks by ordinary mail. I
move around fast. Warmest best wishes to you & Floss,

Hal

W.C. Williams M.D.
9 Ridge Road
Rutherford, N.J.
Sept.13/60

Dear Hal:

"Love Letter" is good. That's the way to do it. "I Have
Wasted My Life" is the wrong lead.
I was amazed to see your name in the roster of
BETWEEN WORLDS and pleased as I could well be.
Neiman has put it well over me with his initiative. It looks
to be a good magazine properly addressed to the new
audience.
We've had a new hurricane over the weekend, trees
down blocking the streets. But today the sun is bright
again as though nothing had occurred. Ain't nature
wonderful? I'm waiting to see the proofs of my five plays
that New Directions has promised for me after the first of
the year.
The Belli sonnets turn out to be only sonnets after all,
your hairy chest notwithstanding; Pound was right, you
shouldn't have printed them if you couldn't have strictly
rhymed them throughout, that would have given them their

only ironic point.

Sincerely yours
Bill

Via S. Maria dell' Anima 49,
Int. 8 Rome, Italy
Sept./Oct. 1960

Dear Bill,

Your last letter flipped me. The Belli sonnets are *not*
unrhymed. Anybody can make a rhyme count if he takes
the trouble. I counted 41 fully or partially rhymed out of
the 46 published. Many are strictly rhymed, others half-
rhymed, assonantal, etc., a common practice. Pound was
wrong. There is something peculiar about your remark that
the sonnets "turn out to be only sonnets after all...Pound
was right..." You've been praising these translations for five
years in letters and personally when I saw you [two] years
ago. Not to mention the preface to the book. What has
happened? It's not just that you seem to have changed your
mind, but it's the way you go about it that throws me.
Also, it was mighty strange, after 8 years of such friendly
correspondence as ours, to see your letter close with
"Sincerely yours". It was the first time you wrote me that
formally, & I'm more than a little astonished & worried. It is
not merely to defend the Belli translations—altho your
remarks leave a very dry taste in my mouth—for many fine
poets have already said extravagant things about how good
they are. It is more to defend our relationship which, for

some reason entirely unknown to me, seems too casually held in your last brief note. If I am to blame in any way, by anything I've said or done, please come out with it. If not, for God's sake, cut out this cold stuff!

Anyway, I'm leaving for France, sometime within the next ten days, and will have no address except AMERICAN EXPRESS, RUE SCRIBE, PARIS, FRANCE. I'm always glad to hear from you. I have some big plans for catching some sort of freighter in February out of Port Said that makes a tour of the whole East before landing in San Francisco, where I will land for a month or two before catching another freighter back to Europe. My mother, at 68, has picked up bag & baggage, left New York where she has lived all her life, & caught a plane to the West Coast where she wants to get a little bungalow or something on her old age pension. So I'll probably be back in the States for a spell, on the other coast.

Best,
Hal

W.C. Williams M.D.
9 Ridge Road
Rutherford, N.J.
Oct. 28/60

Forget it, I had a bad day, that's all. It's surprising that I don't have more of them living the way I have to with so much going on in the family about. If I could I think I would quit an interest in poets entirely .

But don't worry, if you ever do, I'm already mired up to

the armpits, I can't do anything more about it.

Your plans for the future as they involve your hardy Mother sound fascinating. As long as you do not quit writing I hope you'll let me hear from you from time to time. Strange things are still happening in the modern world quite outside the academies—at the same time the conservative bastards now are getting somewhat the upper hand.

Belli had to back up and go into the fold in the end.

Affectionately
Bill

9 Rue Git-le-Coeur
Paris 6, France
6/9/61

Dear Ole Bill,

I've been thinking of you often with great fondness & see no reason why I shouldn't write to say so—especially since we've somehow got out of touch for a while. I saw the Becks' production of your *Many Loves* here in Paris a couple of months ago & liked it immensely. It made me want to write to you at once, but I got sidetracked again. Anyway, here I am. To say hello. I hope you're feeling better again, as Julian Beck said you were having some more trouble. I'd like to hear how you're getting along.

It is over 8 years now since I've been living in Europe, & it looks like I'll be coming back next Spring—if there is another Spring, the way the world is going now, & I mean going. Macmillan is putting out my book of poems that we had a fight over in our famous garden talk of 1958. It is quite a bit changed, a better book, but not the one for you. Ferlinghetti has the fourth one, CLASSIC FRIEZE IN A GARAGE, & you might say that at last I've found my way in these poems, & that garden party of ours was no doubt the chief influence in the turn I took. The poems have been appearing in *Big Table, Between Worlds, Two Cities,* & finally *Evergreen Review* has awakened to my existence. I am beginning to be treated at long last like a real poet. So maybe if I come back in the Spring, I may even give some readings & come onto the scene alive & kicking. My friends who show up here from the States tell me that I really ought to go back & show myself now, because my reputation is growing & I might even get some grants & awards. *Quien sabe?* Stranger things have been known to happen.

Paris no longer has the charm & easy way about her that she used to have. It is all bustle & tension & nerves & bitterness. As I look out my front window onto the street, night & day, I see two suspicious gendarmes staring at everyone. They are guarding the house opposite, where the ex-chief of police has been threatened by the FLN with assassination—plastic bomb. He is on the death list. And if they blow up that house, I guess we get it too. Yet I'm staying on for a while. It takes more than that to scare me off. This is the famous "Beat Hotel" where Corso, Ginsberg & Burroughs live when they're in Paris. They're all in Tangier now. My room is cheap & small, but I like it. I have two tables, one for cooking & one for writing, & a gas stove & two huge wardrobes. Three chairs, a double brass bed & a naked dim light bulb in the center of the room.

Great. Aside from the *flics* when I look out the window I
see the Quai des Grands Augustins & the Seine. Behind us
a bit is Nôtre Dame which I don't see. But there is a patch
of gray sky & some light. Still, the old charm is gone.
Maybe I'm not so young as I used to be—but what with
nuclear explosions, world tension, etc., aren't we all on the
death list? What a life! Maybe tomorrow I'll be blown up
here, & maybe tomorrow we'll all be blown up. The world
has always been in the hands of assassins anyway. Us
poets—we're the dreamy ones! talking about love & rebirth
all the time...even when we're sardonic that's really our
theme. We're born with celebration in our bones. And the
strontium keeps seeping in. Strontium & fallout—what
dirty words! Ugh! What a nasty time. Assassins & swine.
Can't we get rid of *them* once & for all?! For thousands of
years the swine have had it all their way. Swine, jackals,
hyenas, wolves—the herd. Love & rebirth. In the middle
of the herd. When Jesus picked fishermen to initiate into
the mysteries of love & rebirth, he was trying to tell swine
to be men. I guess it didn't work. Swine are swine. After
Jesus came the lawyer Paul & it all turned into the Civil
Service: the Church! And after Karl Marx came the other
intellectual assassin, Lenin, to fight force with force. Swine
with swine. Every vision of utopia ending up in the pigsty
with a nasty blood-bath. Love & rebirth. The brotherhood
of Man. But when will Man appear! He is due! he is due! If
he doesn't appear now, it's all over. It is time for Man to
take over.
     End of homily.
     My warmest regards to you & Floss. Please write if you
feel like it. I'll be at this address about a month. Then off!
I don't know where. I have a little car, Fiat 600, very pretty,

very blue, with white wheels like a blue cat with white paws. It's a dainty car, & I got it in exchange for some of my paintings. You knew that I became a painter some months ago, didn't you? I had a one-man show on the Rue de Seine about a month after I started painting & LIFE MAGAZINE came to take fotos of me & do a story. It hasn't come out yet. *Olé!*

Best,
Hal

W.C. Williams
9 Ridge Road
Rutherford, N.J.
April16/63

Dear Harold:

It was good to hear from you. Bill was glad to go—he had failed so the past year—and was unable to do anything. It was cruel to have wanted him to go on. He had a good, full life—and I'm glad for that.

Do come to see me when you return to the States. I'll be here unless I happen to be away for a time.

Floss

To order additional copies of this book write to:

537 Jones Street
#263
San Francisco, CA 94102

5736

DATE DUE

APR 23 1998	
MAY 1 7 2002	